CULTURE SHOCK!
France

Sally Adamson Taylor

Graphic Arts Center Publishing Company
Portland, Oregon

In the same series

Argentina	Denmark	Japan	South Africa
Australia	Ecuador	Korea	Spain
Austria	Egypt	Laos	Sri Lanka
Belgium	Finland	Malaysia	Sweden
Bolivia	France	Mauritius	Switzerland
Borneo	Germany	Mexico	Syria
Brazil	Greece	Morocco	Taiwan
Britain	Hong Kong	Myanmar	Thailand
California	Hungary	Nepal	Turkey
Canada	India	Netherlands	UAE
Chile	Indonesia	Norway	Ukraine
China	Iran	Pakistan	USA
Costa Rica	Ireland	Philippines	USA—The South
Cuba	Israel	Scotland	Venezuela
Czech Republic	Italy	Singapore	Vietnam

Barcelona At Your Door	New York At Your Door	A Traveler's Medical
Beijing At Your Door	Paris At Your Door	Guide
Chicago At Your Door	Rome At Your Door	A Wife's Guide
Havana At Your Door	San Francisco At Your	Living and Working
Jakarta At Your Door	Door	Abroad
Kuala Lumpur, Malaysia	Tokyo At Your Door	Personal Protection At
At Your Door		Home & Abroad
London At Your Door	A Globe-Trotter's Guide	Working Holidays
Moscow At Your Door	A Parent's Guide	Abroad
Munich At Your Door	A Student's Guide	

Illustrations by TRIGG
Cover photographs by Luca I. Tettoni
Photographs by Sally Taylor and Michelle Brothers

© 1990 Times Editions Pte Ltd
© 2000 Times Media Private Limited
Revised 1993, 1996, 1999, 2003
Reprinted 1997, 1998, 1999, 2000, 2001

This book is published by special
arrangement with Times Media Private Limited
Times Centre, 1 New Industrial Road, Singapore 536196
International Standard Book Number 1-55868-767-X
Library of Congress Catalog Number 90-085619
Graphic Arts Center Publishing Company
P.O. Box 10306 • Portland, Oregon 97296-0306 • (503) 226-2402

Printed in Singapore

CONTENTS

ACKNOWLEDGMENTS

Like most of my generation, I started traveling abroad the summer after my university studies were complete. I've never been quite comfortable at home since. So, I live now in many cultures and love my international life. However, when I first set my native American Anglo-Saxon foot on a Paris sidewalk in 1970, I was so intimidated by the French *hauteur* that I determined to have nothing more to do with that country or those people. Two decades later, I am a total Francophile. Though I still find Parisians difficult at times, I am grateful to live among them. Between hate and love, the French say, there is just one step.

Research for this book really began with that first horrible experience in Paris 25 years ago. In trying to temper my own views with the observations and wisdom of a great many others, it is I who have benefited most from this book.

Of the many who have made personal and intellectual contributions, I would like to particularly thank Sam Abt, my first French teacher Mme Albaugh (wherever she is), Elizabeth Antebi, Adeline & Renaud de Barry, Barbara Bell, Fiona Beeston, Paul Bertier, Isabelle Bolgert, Rebecca Boone, Michele Brothers, Raymonde Carroll, Mouloud Chekini, John & Nona Denis, Nathalie Fieldel-Schact, Therese de Gasquet, Mary de Vachon, Franck Gauthey, Ruth & Lew Goldhammer, Kim Guptill, Gus Hawkins, Neil Hollander, Francis Kelsall, Christy Love, Régine Michel, Robert Moran, Ivy & Chandran Nair, Radha Nair, Polly Platt, Rod Shippey, Janine & Charles Stockton, my mother Ann Adamson Taylor (a pioneer in intercultural relationships), Rob & Neil van der Plas, Susan Wagner, Esther Wanning, and the women at WICE, AAWE and Bloom.

Paris, 1995

I would like to thank my wonderful assistant Christopher Pitts, who did a fine job in researching and updating the information for the 2003 edition of *Culture Shock! France*.

San Francisco, 2003

Chapter One

THE GALLIC ROOSTER

"The French constitute the most brilliant and the most
dangerous nation in Europe and the best qualified in turn
to become an object of admiration, hatred, pity or terror,
but never indifference."

—Alexis de Tocqueville

France has peculiarities that can frustrate anyone, no matter what their
cultural expectations. This book seeks to help explain those peculiarities and why they are "normal" and "reasonable" when you are in
France. We will try to use the noun "international" instead of referring
to non-French people as "foreigners", "tourists" or "expatriates."

Our goal is to show that the cultural realities of France are not in relationship to your own, but unique unto themselves. By accepting these invisible realities, much as you would learn the grammar of the language, you can become as fluent in "French culture" as you can in the language. While one does not preclude the other, each offers the rewards of its own enlightenments.

France has more potential frustrations than most countries, but none offers more pleasures to those who surmount them. This book is designed to help you do that in a number of unique ways. Thousands of books have been written about all that France has to offer. Here we describe what the French expect of themselves, and by default, what they will expect of you. The French have a profound sense of democracy. They believe that all people deserve equal consideration and that individual dignity is important. But like all rest of us they have their own definitions of what is dignified.

They will expect you to understand their "rules" in the same way that you expect people at home to understand yours. In France, you will be accepted immediately as an equal (you are a human being), but you will not be immediately embraced. Don't worry! The French don't immediately embrace each other!

It is always a precarious path, learning what is and what is not acceptable when you go beyond your own cultural boundaries. With this book we hope to remove some of the stumbling blocks for you and even get a wind pushing at your back. Once you learn a few of the "rules", it is safe to say that the more you are "yourself" in France, the more you will be appreciated.

HOW THIS BOOK IS ORGANIZED

In any examination of French life, we must divide our subject into two: public life and private life. The French behave very differently when they have on their "public" form than when they are feeling relaxed and "at home" in private. In each chapter, we will look at how this dichotomy affects the way the French interact with each other. It helps a great deal in understanding the rationality behind their actions. As in all cultures, their reasons for doing things are very rational, but will only appear so when it is clear upon what assumptions each action is taken.

Every interaction involves some form of communication, so we must consider language first. Learning the French language obviously improves anyone's enjoyment of France, but fluency in language is not the same as fluency in culture. In fact, there are many "non-verbal" ways in which we all communicate and I have seen some people who are very good at non-verbal communication enjoy the subtleties of Paris and travel throughout the country without speaking more than a few words of the language.

In general, though, a good conversation in France involves language and ideas. We will look at various aspects of French history, art and politics and see how they affect the ways the French see themselves and the world.

This book is a kind of cultural road map, examining the various points at which you will first interact with the French and suggesting ways to make these points of contact positive and enlightening. It is people, not only museums and architecture, that make a country.

We will look particularly at the important topics of food and wine, of shopping and street life. Then, we will try to get behind closed doors for a look at the home life of France, a world you may not have many chances to see on your first visits. This section will help prepare you for being both a thoughtful resident and a repeat guest.

The final sections of the book only scratch the surface of their topics. There are complete books written now, on dealing with the business place and with various aspects of the French law and pragmatics. Our Practical Information section will lead you to further reading on these subjects and we've compiled a bibliography of further sources. Throughout the chapters, we've include cultural perspectives wherever possible of why the French do a certain thing a certain way. You will finish this book thinking more like a French man AND a French woman, because the sexes have cultural differences of their own.

The back of the book features several appendices: "culture shock" clinically defined and various sources to help cope with it; the equally difficult task of going home and the bibliography mentioned above.

This book is only a broad sketch of French culture, but we hope the insights you gain here will bring you more quickly to appreciate those most remarkable and wonderful people, the French ...

The First Step: Survival Tips

> "... we are caught between the desire to deny differences
> (we are all human) and the desire to emphasize them (the
> right to be different)."
> —Raymonde Carroll, *Cultural Misunderstandings*

There are certain basics of cultural survival in any country, like eating, dressing and communicating. In France, each of these is an art form. To be able to speak some French, enough to communicate basic needs and desires, will make a tremendous difference in getting you started with life in France.

Most French people are very tolerant of poor French and once you've tried to reach out, they will reach out, too, with their (what they consider to be) poor English. The section on "Learning French" gives you a starting point with the French language, if you haven't started already. Persevere! You'll be challenged and rewarded time and again when you are in France, if you keep trying.

The dress code in France appears to be typically western and, especially among the young, "anything goes". But you will also find, especially when in Paris, that the French say a great deal with the way they dress. As in many major cities in the world, the men dress in business suits for work and the women dress "up" for work. The streets are full of people for whom being sophisticated includes dressing the part.

Of course you can wear comfortable old running shoes and that baggy running gear you slept in on the plane when you go to the Louvre. But if you have the slightest concern about sticking out as a tourist-with-the-fashion-sense-of-a-barbarian, you won't.

When in Paris, do as the Parisians. Enjoy the art and the food and your own participation in this remarkable city in clothes that make you feel good about yourself. The French don't care what you wear. At the opera you'll find everything from full length gowns with diamond tiara to blue jeans and T-shirts. But everyone will admire a well assembled outfit, a person who looks his best and knows it. It's not a question of the latest expensive style or uncomfortable but dressy shoes. It's your own best taste. Just remember, Paris is not Disneyland. That is still a train-ride away.

Eating. Ah, here is your daily reward for coping with the complexities of France. The endless joy of the French is their food. Menus are studied in detail. Waiters are proud of their role and advise on choices as seriously as a doctor gives a prognosis. Two hours are often dedicated to the pleasures of a single meal. The only thing you can do really "wrong" with French food is rush it.

The Next Step: Understanding Cultural Differences

Culture shock can be reduced considerably if you know something of how the French see themselves, both in public life and in private life. A little later we will "put paid" to those dreadful things, cultural stereotypes. Like any truisms, cultural stereotypes have some truth in them, but real understanding goes beyond stereotypes and cultural understanding is the lifelong enrichment of travel. So the international quickly learns to ignore these stereotypes.

Among the many helpful sources for this book, the insights of Raymonde Carroll in *Cultural Misunderstandings* have been my biggest inspiration. A French woman trained as an anthropologist and married to an American, Dr. Carroll has developed an excellent approach to avoiding false assumptions when studying cultural attitudes.

Cultural analysis is an act of humility, says Dr. Carroll, in which you attempt to forget, for a moment, your own way of seeing and briefly replace it with another way, knowing you can never adopt that other way, only assert its validity. One can live a long time in another culture and never understand it. It is too easy to treat opaque situations as if they were transparent, and thus never really understanding them. Like the process of learning another language, cultural understanding is difficult and sometimes painful. But the more you learn, the more perceptive you become.

Raymonde Carroll explains, "... one of the great advantages of cultural analysis, aside from that of expanding our horizons, is that of transforming our cultural misunderstandings from a source of occasionally deep wounds into a fascinating and inexhaustible exploration of the other."

Sounds like personal relationships, doesn't it?

Let's Meet the French

Too often one hears people say that they love France, but hate the French. To them, we offer the retort of American Parisian and Francophile, Gertrude Stein: "How can foreigners say they like France but not the French? It's the French who made the France they like – and it is the French who keep it that way."

Everyone with a western education arrives in France armed with a certain knowledge of the government, economics, politics, religion, history and national character of France. All this is part of our international heritage and it should come as no surprise that the French believe in their cultural superiority.

The French use a rooster as their national symbol. This play on words probably began 2,000 years ago as the Latin word for France, "Gaul", also means "rooster" in Latin. The French readily admit their tendencies towards self-promotion, crowing and strutting like a rooster in the barnyard. They laugh at this weakness in themselves. But the world cannot but admire the way the French have promoted their wines, perfumes and fashion houses to the world. They know marketing!

Way back in 1787, Horace Walpole complained of the French "insistent airs of superiority." Remember that for 200 years, all civilized people in the western world spoke and read French. International business and diplomacy were conducted nearly exclusively in French up until the World War I.

"Foreigners have to remind themselves they are not dealing with a country that really exists ... but with a country that most Frenchmen dream still exists," says Luigi Barzini is his book *The Europeans*. "The gap between the two is a large one," he admits. "But the French indefatigably try to ignore it or forget it."

Charles de Gaulle, leader of the French Resistance during World War II and beloved president of France in the 1960s, perpetuated the perception that France leads the world down the path of mankind. "*La France est la lumière du monde, son génie est d'illuminer l'Univers* (France is the light of the world, her genius lights the universe)," he said. Even in 1981, when François Mitterand accepted the job of President, he said, "A just and generous France ... can light the path of mankind." The French still love to hear it and many of us Francophiles have come to believe it. France greets more visitors each year than her total population. She, indeed, has a mission to civilize. In spite of a century that has not been kind to France, Paris is still indisputably the most architecturally beautiful city in the world.

World War I destroyed nearly two million of the brightest and best of the French male population and the years leading up to World War II did not revive the French economy or her spirit. France had the oldest population in Europe when in 1939 the nation was forced to surrender to the vastly superior technologies of the invading Germans. World War II still lives in the memories of many French people as a time of disgrace under German domination. The four years of Occupation must have seemed like the death knell to French culture, to all that the French hold dear.

The liberation in 1944 gave the French back their hope. In spite of disastrous wars in Indochina and Algeria following World War II, France recovered both spiritually and economically under the Fifth Republic, established by de Gaulle in 1956.

There are 57 million French people today; 90% still call themselves Roman Catholic, but only 12% of Christians go to church. The country is only 213,000 square miles (547,000 km^2), but in the Paris area alone, there are 10 million people, two million inside the city proper. Included in this 10 million are 40% of the 20 to 25-year-olds. Thus the countryside's population density is quite low (101 people per km^2) and elderly.

The French identity extends to outposts (former colonies) all over the world. These *Départments d'Outre-Mer* (DOM) and *Territoires d'Outre-Mer* (TOM) are legally part of France and their people philosophically French, though they do experience elements of racial discrimination when they come to mother France.

Maintaining an exquisite but aging capital city with the highest level of taxation in Europe, France enjoys a mix of the traditional, the exotic, and the latest technological advances. Old Paris is served by the Concorde and the high-speed TGV trains, both the fastest in the world and both French-made. France was the third country in the world to develop a nuclear bomb and about 65% of her energy needs are supplied by nuclear power plants scattered around the country.

Yet Parisians still demand the freshest farm vegetables and purest wines. A constant theme in conversation is the deterioration of the quality of life, while everywhere around the visitor, its evidences seem certain.

The Regional Diversity

"How can you govern, in peacetime, a people with 365 different cheeses?" de Gaulle asked. The Frenchman answered, "How can you live in a country without them?"

One of the most fascinating inconsistencies of France is her regional diversity. Paris is as much like the rest of France as New York is like the rest of the USA, yet each region is also unique. The French love of food and wine reflects their attachment to this diversity. Later, we offer a thumbnail sketch of each region in the context for which each is best known by other Frenchmen: what they eat and what they drink.

Only one in two Parisians was born in Paris. Many keep homes or have family living in the countryside. In spite of being an urban population the French retain a love of the land and return regularly there to enjoy it, though not to work, as a small fraction of the population now feeds the whole.

We really focus on the cultural aspects of Paris in this book. This is the part of France most internationals need to know and Paris is the most complex aspect of French life. People in the countryside are more friendly, more patient and more relaxed. We focus on Paris, yet hope to describe the France Louis Barzini calls "a unique, lively, inventive, restless, courageous, brilliant and disquieting country."

Chapter Two

IN A STRANGE LAND

"*Ce qu'il y a de plus étranger en France, pour les Français, c'est la France.*" (What is most foreign in France, for the French, is France.)

—Balzac, *Modeste Mignon*

All of us who travel and make friends in other nations quickly learn the pitfalls of cultural stereotypes and even cultural generalizations. It is easy but pointless to rage against the "illogical" differences between your logic and someone else's. Conversely, who wants to be "pigeon-holed" as someone "typical" of his own culture? Each of us takes pride in our own individuality, yet all of us are guilty of misjudging others by applying cultural stereotypes.

Though generalizations are unavoidable in this book, we are going to try to get beyond the most overbearing and inaccurate ones. There are some elements of truth in any cultural stereotype, some valid reasons why they were formed, even if the conclusions made from the observations are a stretch. Rather than ignoring the monster, let us examine some of the stereotypes now, both those you may have heard about the French and those the French may have about you.

If culture is an onion, we are starting with that dry brown paper skin. It tells you very little about the character of what you will find inside, but you have to get beyond it first. Knowing a little bit about how you are being seen may also help you understand the person looking at you. But please keep in mind: stereotypes are, at very best, only a place to start, not to stop, on the road to cultural understanding.

No need to be thin skinned about any of this. We all have superficial cultural biases to discard. So with apologies to every French person I ever met, here are some of the cultural stereotypes that have formed about the French.

STEREOTYPES ABOUT THE FRENCH

"An Englishman apologizes when you step on his foot. A Frenchman berates you when he steps on yours."
—Mort Rosenblum, *Mission to Civilize*

For centuries, the French have stereotyped themselves using the symbol of the rooster: not only does he crow loudly and pointlessly, he holds himself aloof from the other animals in the barnyard. He considers himself superior to all who neglect to challenge his authority, which is laughable, but he gets away with it by posturing.

The Gallic temperament has been stereotyped as cold, imperious and negative. The French do joke about it. *Le pire est toujours certain* ("The worst is always a certainty") is a favorite French expression.

To a bubbly, enthusiastic American or a polite and sensitive Asian, the typical French public behavior is often interpreted as a personal rebuff. This behavior has nothing to do with anyone else, we will soon find. That cool way the French have of dealing with public life is the flip side of their genuine warmth and humor, which is saved for their friends and family (and a few oddball things like pets and people on crutches).

The French do not hate foreigners. You will see in the next part of this chapter that they generally prefer people of other nations to their own countrymen. However, they tend to resist getting involved with strangers, especially French strangers.

That public coolness that is so off-putting can also flip over suddenly into heated participation, especially if a French person senses an insult. This creates another stereotype about the French: that they are argumentative and confrontational. I once saw a very elderly and refined-looking French lady in the *métro* suddenly start beating

a young man with her umbrella while she screamed obscenities at him, accusing him of grabbing at her purse.

In a traffic jam, it won't take long before a honking, shouting and fist-waving competition begins among the drivers. Yet the French will rarely come to serious physical violence – remember the rooster ...

The French love to argue. They call it "discussion". In Roman times, Tacitus reported that if the Gauls hadn't quarreled so much among themselves, they wouldn't have been defeated. But this quarreling also has a healthy and positive direction to it, which will be discussed in detail in the section on "The Art of Conversation" in the following chapter.

In general, a French person will strive to maintain his composure, his *amour propre*, in public. He will admire you for doing the same, though it may appear at first he is trying to throw you off-balance with his unsmiling reserve.

To see the more positive side of this uncontrollable Gallic hot-and-cold, take a puppy for a walk on any street in Paris and watch that cool, elegantly dressed French woman drop to her knees to slobber gurgles of adoration on the animal. These strong shifts of mood and temper have a wonderful effect in France: they keep everyone from getting bored. More than anything, a Frenchman hates to be bored.

"Flee boredom," advised Coco Chanel. "It's fattening."

"They cannot bear being bored," said Alphonse de Lamartine of his countrymen in 1847. And they rarely are. Nor will you be.

Beyond Gauls & Franks

Because most of the French are conservative stay-at-homes, there are still strong regional differences. Though the ancient peoples of France, Gallic and Frankish, have flocked to the urban centers in recent years, they visit home often, and retain their regional characteristics in their cuisine.

We will consider them, stereotypically gastronomically, in the section on French regional cooking. The more recent racial and cultural additions to the make-up of France concern us now. France went out into the world with a mission to civilize that started with the Christian Crusades in the Middle Ages. This "civilizing", which continues today, is examined in detail in an excellent book *Mission to Civilize* by Mort Rosenblum. (All books we mention appear in the Bibliography.)

In her history, France has admitted as many immigrants as Australia, from all parts of the globe. Each culture bears a different relationship to the rest. The French do not like to think of themselves as racist. Tolerance for religious differences was first codified in France by King Henry IV with the Edict of Nantes in 1598, though there were brutal efforts later to maintain the dominance of the Roman Catholic Church.

In the following century, when colonization began in earnest, the French had to cope with more than religious differences. By the time of the French Revolution, France had her fair share of colonies around the globe, and in true democratic spirit, extended the privileges of being free and equal in France. They were quite shocked, therefore, when many of these colonies chose independence over French citizenship when given the choice. The Algerian War in the 1960s was a particularly unhappy lesson for France.

In the last century, France has lost most of her possessions abroad, leaving small pieces scattered around the world that amount to little, in terms of numbers. But true to their democratic principles, the French still extend to these people equal status. Every French citizen living abroad is represented in the French legislature. There are even two representatives of the French living in the USA!

The French populations of the world can be educated as French citizens, using the same curricula, and they can move freely between Europe and their homes (referred to as DOM, *Départements d'Outre Mer* and TOM, *Territoires d'Outre Mer*). Many have chosen to live in France. North African, black African, Middle Eastern and Asian peoples in France enjoy all the privileges of French citizenship, but are hampered these days by underlying racial prejudices related to high unemployment in France.

Political immigrants fare far better, as the French take pride in extending asylum to all those with radical ideas found unpopular elsewhere. Thus, both the Ayatollah Khomeini and the Shah of Iran have called France home during their respective bouts of unpopularity at home. France has been described as a conservative country that is tolerant of extremes. Up to 1962, the major foreign presence in France was the Italians, followed by the Spaniards, though Poles, Russians, Armenians and Hungarians had also come to France in large numbers (over 250,000 of each) during various political upheavals in their own countries in the middle of this century. Many of these people eventually assimilated into French culture.

However, racially different French people tend to remain near the bottom of the socio-economic ladder. Since the independence of Algeria, a French colony until 1962, the major foreign residents in France have been, first, the Algerians, followed by the Portuguese.

Today, 10% of the population of France is Muslim, nearly all of them North Africans. The French refer to all Muslims as Arabs, and the connotation is not very positive. The children of these former Algerians and Moroccans, those born in France, are called "Beurs". They are French-speaking and French-educated, but still racially distinguishable and socially separated.

In Paris, racial minorities tend to group together. The North Africans, the black Africans and the Asians (mostly Vietnamese and Chinese) tend to cluster in the 13th, 18th, 19th and 20th *arrondissements* of Paris. In spite of a generally democratic view towards people, the large and visible populations of "outsiders" in Paris has bred some resentment among the older French population, especially since political turmoil in the Arab world has resulted in the bombing of innocent French citizens.

Especially critical of the Arabs are those who feel they are competing for jobs and paying out of their taxes for the health care, schools and other social services provided every French person, employed or not. Some French people even stereotype the Arabs as aggressive and untrustworthy.

People of other former colonies of France, particularly the dark-skinned peoples of West Africa, the West Indies and the South Pacific, generally fare better in France than in many other predominantly white countries. French-speaking blacks are generally considered gentle and easy-going by their compatriots. American blacks are idolized for their musical abilities as black American musicians are usually the only blacks the French see.

Many whose homelands have established independence are still considered French citizens, including the people of Guadeloupe, Guyana, Martinique, Reunion, New Caledonia and Polynesia. French Asians from Vietnam, Cambodia and China are considered honest and hard-working and have less difficulty as a race integrating with French culture, as they have cultural heritages greatly admired by the French.

In spite of some racial tensions, you will see many "mixed" couples in France. Children of all racial backgrounds enjoy the public parks and museums together in general harmony.

There is some anti-Semitism in some circles in France, which may help explain some feelings of racial difference Jewish people may exhibit here, with both pride and defensiveness.

YOUR TURN TO BE STEREOTYPED

The French may have certain, immediate stereotypical reactions to you, based on your foreign origin, or just on the fact that you are a tourist, at least until you can establish yourself as an individual.

Being a tourist is the first stereotype you'll want to try to shake. Even if your French is good, your accent will quickly pigeon-hole you. To fly this nest, see the next chapter on non-verbal communication, and from there continue to the section on fashion. If you are a French Canadian, you can explain yourself and get a warm, brotherly welcome, if your accent hasn't already done that for you. Otherwise, don't be surprised to be lumped with others of your homeland and judged by these generalities:

The Americans from the USA

An American from the USA, as opposed to a Canadian, is considered something of a conformist by the French, both in dress and in values (tourists in running shoes, blue jeans and a backpack looking for souvenir postcards and T-shirts). They are naive (easy pickpocket victims), very loud in restaurants, and ruthlessly power-hungry in business. Americans seem primarily interested in making money and in how much everything costs, boasting about their achievements in both areas. The French are confused by the weak American family ties, so unstructured and haphazard.

Many French people complain that Americans quickly become boring because they like everything superficially and understand nothing in depth. Enthusiasm is not a requirement in France; comprehension is. A happy-face smile is the mark of an idiot in France, or worse. Yet basically the French like Americans. They like the enthusiasm (in moderation) and the informality of Americans. The young even dress and act like American film stars. But they don't understand why Americans think the French don't like Americans.

The British & other English-speakers

The animosity and wars between France and England go back into the mists of time, though they did stick together in both World Wars. Though much common blood flows between the two peoples, now there is still plenty of mutual ribbing between the French and the English.

Stereotypes among the French paint the British as cold, insensitive, perfidious and stingy, with no sense of passion. An English person will invite you to dinner once, they say, then never again. A

23

French person may take a year to invite you, but after that, they will include you forever in their circle. But since the British cuisine is considered so inferior, perhaps that's not so bad. While over six million Britons visit France each year, only two million French visit Britain, so there is clear consensus regarding the superiority of French cuisine.

The Australians bear the Crocodile Dundee image, but they are often confused with loud Midwestern Americans. Heavy drinking groups of young Australians win few points among the French, who are intolerant of obvious inebriation.

The English Canadians, with their strong historical connections with France, are slotted as French provincials, even if they don't speak the language. The French Canadians are closer still, even though they don't speak French properly.

The Asians

Non-French Asians are assumed to be polite, very intelligent, hard-working and non-aggressive, except concerning money matters, just like the French Asians. Yet the Asian habit of keeping one's distance and not showing one's feelings (at least not in ways a French person can understand) is interpreted as being cold and hypocritical. The Asian smile that expresses discomfort and embarrassment is often misinterpreted as ingratiating.

Until the Japanese started coming in great numbers and spending a great deal of money, few French people distinguished among different Asian peoples, even though Vietnam was once a French colony. They tended to group all "yellow" people together. That Chinese cuisine is acknowledged as one of the world's best helps Asian internationals in France, even though most Chinese food in France has been badly adulterated to please the French palate.

The French also share with the Asians strong family links. French writer Paul Morand compared the French and the Chinese in his book *Hiver Caraïbe* at the beginning of this century:

"There is a striking likeness between the Chinese and ourselves, the same passion for economy by making things last, by repairing them endlessly, the same genius for cooking, the same caution and old world courtesy, an inveterate but passive hatred of foreigners, conservatism tempered by social gales, lack of public spirit and the same indestructible vitality of old people who have passed the age of illness. Should we not think that all ancient civilizations have much in common?"

The Japanese

Japan is now the major market for the best French food, wine, fashion, perfume, jewelry and technology. Japanese tourists are ubiquitous in the most elegant shopping districts of Paris and Japanese is widely written and spoken here.

There is both a fascination and a threat in things Japanese. French intellectuals love Japanese aesthetics: movies, literature and traditional arts, yet the Japanese reputation for copying technology and endlessly taking photographs is suspect. The way they flock to Japanese restaurants in Paris is also curious. However, the Japanese are considered hard-working and dignified, especially in their Gucci shoes and Chanel suits.

Other Cultures in General

Though they have other stereotypes of Europeans, in general, the French distinguish little among other people, as culturally different from themselves. This is to your advantage. The French judge, and expect to be judged, as individuals. Therefore, we hope you consider the views expressed in this chapter the shallowest part of the book. From here on, we shall try to delve more deeply into the French culture, and get beyond these superficial stereotypes.

Chapter Three

PARLEZ-VOUS FRANÇAIS?

NON-VERBAL COMMUNICATION

To learn anything about a culture, you have to communicate, and the most basic form of communication is non-verbal. We all know people with no language skills who get along great wherever they go. They have great intuitive non-verbal skills. You can get a long way if you are blessed with these.

But if you aren't, you can get into trouble in a hurry by miscommunicating or misunderstanding the rules of French non-verbal communication. So let us introduce some of the basics.

Eye Contact

Making eye-contact is a serious statement of equality in France. It is a recognition of the other person's identity and is considered too personal for use with strangers. Generally, avoid eye contact when walking down the street, especially if you are a woman.

If you look directly into a stranger's eyes on the street or in a café, for example, that will construed as a request for intimacy, a "pick-up" in the American vernacular.

As a man, however, you have the "right" to toss a look at a woman whom you find attractive. Polly Platt calls this "the Look" in her book *French or Foe?* and every woman who comes to France quickly becomes aware of it. Take it as a compliment, but don't return it and don't smile unless you want to progress to the next level with that person. More on smiling in a minute.

Refusing to make eye contact gives you distance. (This also works when driving an automobile, as we will see later.) On the other hand, refusing to make eye contact with someone you are dealing with directly is a "put down", especially if that person is your waiter or shop attendant. To appear genuine, establish some brief eye contact, especially with people who are supposed to be helping you. You will get a far better response.

The Smile

If you are American, this is going to be your single biggest non-verbal miscommunication when in France. The tendency of Americans is to smile all the time, to appear friendly and reasonable. The French do not trust a smile. If they can see no apparent reason for it, it smacks of hypocrisy, a very unpleasant thing to a French person. English and Asian readers will understand this French reticence about smiling quite easily.

I am a Californian. I smile automatically. I look better when I smile and I feel better. But in France I constantly remind myself to wipe that smile off my face as I walk down the street just happy to be

27

French is a lovely language which is full of musicality. But the French people also use their whole body to convey meanings.

in Paris. It gives the wrong message. It makes people nervous, if I do. Am I an idiot, they wonder? Am I laughing at their expense?

While I love France and I love being there, I know that a constant smile on my face will not convey my appreciation. Don't get me wrong – you can smile a lot when in France. But not until you break that public shield and get involved with someone specific for a specific reason.

You don't smile at a stranger on the street and say "hello" just to be friendly. If a construction worker whistles at you or a stranger gives you "the Look" or a street person asks you for money, your lack of expressing keeps the situation neutral and dignified. It is your best response.

There is a wonderful example of this in Polly Platt's book *French or Foe?* where she recalls showing some French executives a picture of their then-President Mitterand at an informal meeting in Texas, smiling. Nobody recognized him! He never smiles for the cameras in France, or at least they don't publish those shots.

This is not to say the French do not smile or that smiles aren't important. The French love to smile, and do so very quickly, as soon as a reason to do so has been established. More on that in the section on conversation.

The Reverse Kiss

The French make a "poof" sound, at the same time blowing air out of their mouth and protracting their lips. That means "it's nothing", either negative or positive, depending on the situation and context. It's currently a very popular expression and one of many non-verbal means of communication you will find.

Using the Fingers and Hands

When counting in Europe, "one" is the thumb. The index finger and thumb extended together means "two". So putting up an index finger to mean "one" is confusing to French people. Do you mean "one" (the thumb) or "two" (the thumb and index finger)? Don't snap your fingers at a person, anywhere. That is considered rude and condescending.

The French love to speak with their hands. Here is some of the more common vocabulary:

- One or several fingers circling at the temple means "that guy is crazy" (*dingue*) and is usually accompanied by a goofy expression.
- Holding one's nose with the fist and faking a turn indicates "that guy is drunk." (*Il est saoul.*)
- Kissing the tips of one's fingers means "delicious", whether it is the food at table or a woman walking down the street.
- Pulling the right cheek downward at the eye, with the right hand means, "I don't believe it." (Lit. *mon œil* as in "my foot".)
- The "OK" circle made with the tip of the thumb and index fingers touching also means "excellent", especially if accompanied by a pucker of the lips.
- Likewise, thumbs down means bad. Thumbs up means Super!
- A hand wiped across the forehead or just above the hairline means "I've had it up to here." (*J'en ai ras-le-bol.*)
- Using the back of the fingers to stroke the right cheek as if it were a beard means *Quelle barbe* or "What a bore."
- The finger tips rubbed together, with the thumb up, as if one were feeling fabric, means "Expensive".
- The fingers together, all reaching skyward, means "I'm afraid" or "he's afraid." (Lit. "Soft balls, we can feel them.") With the reverse kiss, the "poof", it is contemptuous commentary roughly equivalent to "screw you".
- That same "poof" with a hand throwing something over the opposite shoulder means, "It's nothing; I'm above this."
- Making a fist with the right hand and stretching out that arm, then "breaking" it at the elbow with the left wrist is equivalent, in other places, to raising one's middle finger. (*Va te faire foutre*! or "Get stuffed!")

- Making a fist and shaking it leisurely in front of one's chest is often used by men to mean "He's a jerk", and is really an imitation of "jerking off".
- The fingers flat against the lips with eyes open means, "Oops, I made a mistake." No verbal comment is necessary.
- Shaking the fingers of the right hand in front of the chest means great surprise and excitement, positive or negative, and is appropriately accompanied by an "Ooh, la, la!"
- Both hands up in front of the chest, palms out, with a shrug means "I don't know" or "Hey, it's not my job."
- Raising the shoulders, the classic French shrug, means "This is ridiculous."

You will find many more of these, as the French constantly speak non-verbally. It is a wonderful part of their Mediterranean heritage and great drama to watch on the street or at a café. That's why putting one's hands in one's pockets is considered impolite, especially when in conversation. And that is probably also why the handshake is so important.

Shaking Hands

The French shake hands with everyone they know, unless they kiss them, instead (see "The Double Kiss"). It's not a strong handshake, in the gripper American-style, with a long, serious moment of eye contact. It's a brief holding of the hands with an even briefer visual acknowledgement, but it is most important as a French greeting.

Children are taught to shake hands from the time they can walk. Yet at first, it can be most aggravating, this business of handshaking, especially in offices and banks. I've gone to my bank first thing in the morning and watched an endless round of handshake greetings amongst the bank staff behind the counter. I watch helplessly, hoping at some point my teller will be able to free his hands and attention long enough to get on with his job. But this is part of his job! Each employee is obliged to make a handshaking round to every other employee both on arrival and on departure. In a small office with 20 employees ... that's 800 handshakes each day! Comparing such counterproductive formalities with the rush to serve customers in places like Hong Kong, one wonders how the French have managed to retain one of the world's strongest economies.

You will soon become accustomed to the handshake, and soon be able to imitate the lightness of touch and eye-contact required. When you do get into a handshaking situation yourself, whether at work or in company, be sure not to exclude anyone, even if you don't know them.

The Double Kiss

Between friends who are greeting or parting, a kiss on both cheeks is normal, even in public. Again, if there is a group, you should be sure to include everyone, even if you don't really know them, treating them as family. Don't panic. This is not usually expected in business and certainly not between businessmen, only between women, between men and women, between adults and children and between men who are members of the same family.

This is a tough one for the Asians and Anglo-Saxons not accustomed to facial contact with any but our most intimate circle. I find myself more comfortable with this exercise the longer I stay in France and have tried to carry the habit home with me, with some success. Among women, particularly, it is an enjoyable expression of affection, once the technique is perfected. One starts with the right cheeks touching, usually. But if the other person seems bound and determined to go for the left cheek first, for heaven's sake make that one available instead. Otherwise you may smash into each other's mouths, a painful and embarrassingly intimate error.

Most foreigners, myself included, have reduced the intimacy of the double kiss by "kissing the air", instead of actually touching lips to cheek. Given our anatomical design, only one of the two people can actually get their mouth in contact with the other's cheek each time, anyway. So most of us let the French friend make that contact, if they choose. Many French also use this "kissing the air" technique.

Extra touches express greater affection, one assumes. Three touches, alternating cheeks each time, is show of further intimacy and not unusual in Paris. Parisian women will even extend it to four with their women friends, which is gilding the lily a bit.

Whole Body Language

French women and men, especially Parisians, have a reputation for being stunningly good-looking. I've been amazed to find that, in fact, they aren't really particularly beautiful, by Hollywood standards. Their skin may be poor or their teeth bad. They may look tired around the eyes and many French women never bother with make-up.

What gives the French an aura of beauty is the way they present themselves. They hold their bodies erect and they are conscious of themselves as extensions of their whole personality. Like actors, they make their bodies convey whatever message they feel appropriate. The usual messages are: "I am intelligent/sincere/well-raised." It works. In this way, they convey an inner beauty.

It doesn't hurt, of course, that some Parisians are horrified by the prospect of getting fat and diet religiously and walk everywhere, so they do look good in the beautiful and expensive clothes they wear. But others convey elegance and a sense of themselves in blue jeans.

I am also surprised to find how few are more than vaguely aware of this powerful performance their body language presents. This proper carriage and the importance of presentation is taught at an early age and is everywhere apparent. It is second nature to the French to look good, whatever they wear, and thereby convey who they are.

An international quickly becomes aware of this and more conscious, in turn, of the way he is dressed and the way his body conveys messages. We have a section on "Fashion" and its importance in public life, but the whole body language of the French really conveys the message. You will find yourself imitating in short order.

I've seen women on the street who looked totally, typically, elegantly French, and found, as we passed, they were speaking English with American accents! Of course, they did not wear baggy running suits, clunky running shoes and hang big, messy backpacks over themselves, like so many American tourists. But hey, I've also seen Frenchmen and women dress elegantly in running suits.

To convey your own "best" whole body language, come to France in clothes that make you feel good about yourself. Walk tall. Reserve your smiles for people you deal with directly. You'll pick up the finer points as you go along.

Touching

The other "whole body" language that the French use is touching. They touch each other to express friendship rather than any physical desire. This is reserved for friends, of course, but close physical contact can be expected in crowded places in Paris. Just watch for pick pockets in such conditions and if a stranger purposely touches you, give a really nasty "poof" or just ignore him completely, and keep walking, head held high.

THE ART OF CONVERSATION

"However slight the subject the soul is offered, it tends to enlarge the matter and draw it out to the point where it needs to labor at it with all its force."

—Montaigne, *Essais*

An innate restlessness in the French and a love of diversity are satisfied best by lengthy conversation, usually in the structure of analysis. Everywhere you go, you have a chance to practice speaking French and learning things at the same time.

Whether you are passing time in a café or just buying envelopes, expect a discussion of the options. In fact, to invite one, just ask a question. (You can start with Polly Platt's 10 magic words: "*Excusez-*

*moi de vous déranger, Monsieur/Madame, mais j'ai une problème
…")*

I am amazed at the details I have learned about something as
mundane as envelopes and their various glues, just by showing an
interest in the salesperson's opinion. Be it the choice of stationery, the
fruits in season or world politics, contrasts and detail challenge the
French intellect and heighten self-esteem.

The French love nothing better than to be asked their opinion on
a subject they feel strongly about. Yes, the French are "argumentative" but an argument in this case has the legal English meaning here:
it is a point of view presented, not an unpleasant attack.

Compromise, on the other hand, has a negative meaning in
French. It is to be avoided. Far better to end a discussion with all points
made than find some pathetic bit of common ground with which to
stand together. The French are quick to criticize everybody and
everything, but that is often only to make an opportunity for discussion, to "break the ice", so to speak. Most good conversations start
with a complaint and end with a satisfactory display of analytical
thinking. Waiters love to discuss the nuances of their menus. Plumbers the fine points of their trade, and businessmen the extent of their
understanding of the workings of the world.

People who complain that the French talk too much are probably
the same ones who say the French are cool and uncommunicative:
both generalities miss the point. The art of conversation in France is
highly developed. It follows very specific rules. But as a foreigner
with limited skills in French, you will be forgiven a multitude of sins,
as long as you don't commit the only cardinal sin: refusing to
converse.

In France, to enter a shop without saying *Bonjour Madame* or
Bonjour Monsieur to the proprietor or clerk in attendance, acknowledging them as another human being, would be considered very rude.

In England or America, it would be considered unusual, a bit
forward even. It is an important habit to develop in France, no matter

what your other limitations in the language. Always say *Bonjour* and make eye contact if you can. If you can then continue the conversation with a description of what you are looking for, all the better.

No matter what transpires, never leave the shop without a *Merci* and *Au revoir* to these same people. You are acknowledging them as "hosts" in a way; you are in their domain and should respect the relationship that exists between you by the mere fact of your walking into their establishment. Even if you are "just looking".

Silence and its Preserves

Silence can also be appropriate in France, especially among strangers. Silence preserves, the French say. It allows polite distance between people in a public place. Neighbors in a building will respect each others' privacy by maintaining silence as they wait together on the ground floor for the lift (but only after they have acknowledged each other with a *Bonjour Madame* or *Monsieur*). They may go no further than this in their relationship for years!

In a train compartment with six seats, silence will be maintained among the passengers after acknowledgement of their presence. If there is a conversation between two friends among the six, it will be conducted as quietly as possible, out of respect for others' privacy, i.e. their right to silence.

Silence and an expressionless face are neutral and is maintained until human contact is made. It is hard for an American not to smile when he is just walking down the street on a sunny autumn day. Americans are taught to smile, no matter what. The French are not taught that. They need a reason to smile.

In line at a grocery store, if the wait is overlong, the French will make body motions indicating their impatience and they may throw a look of exasperation at other customers in the line for confirmation of the situation, but they will almost never speak. They would be horrified by those Americans who tell their most intimate life details to anybody who will listen at the check-out counter.

Beyond Bonjour

While silence preserves, it can also mean hostility. To pass an acquaintance on the street or to bump into other parents at pick-up time at school without exchanging a small conversation would be considered rude in France. Just *Bonjour* is not enough. A few comments about some topic of interest you share in common, and sensitive to the time limitations of each, is expected. The same for exchanging business with a shopkeeper you know well. *Bonjour* is not enough. *Ça va?* at least, should follow.

In a restaurant, by making the appropriate introductory comments to your waiter, asking his advice on the special dishes of the day, explaining your interest in the cuisine, you can quickly establish a rapport that will turn the evening into a pleasurable cultural plunge, with refreshing insights into both the individuals and the cuisine.

This is not idle chitchat, but a subtle development of interpersonal relations. Your conversational artistry can change the most sour waiter into a friendly one, almost immediately (See the section on "Getting Respect").

Such small conversations, professional exchanges between yourself and the person with whom you are doing business, reflect on both the status and the humanity of the two of you. Conversation, where appropriate, is a great equalizer. It can neutralize an antagonistic (i.e. fearful-of-being-put-down) atmosphere. Your success as a conversant in France can be measured by the harmony of feelings you have accumulated at the end of the day.

Starting Conversations with Strangers

Diversity creates dialogue and analysis, great sources of pleasure in France. People participate with sincerity and energy in conversation. It is a skill and an art. Conversation commits people, forms a temporary bond. It is important. You can get plenty of practice in the art of French conversation once you've established yourself as a willing interlocutor, even if your French is poor.

You'll find plenty of seemingly "non-communicative" French people happy to talk to you, with the proper approach. The French are most at ease when they are in conversation. They want to express their opinions. They just need the opportunity to get started.

We've already explained that French conversation in public among strangers is usually limited to exchanges between customers and shopkeepers. To go into a café and start talking to another customer could easily be considered an invasion of his or her privacy, or even a proposition for sex on your part.

Your best bet at a bar or in a café or shop is to wait until other customers have been presented to you through the waiter, bartender or clerk. If you are with a group, or they are, that makes your advances easier, as your motives are clearly innocent.

People sitting at a table next to you may themselves start a conversation with you, especially once they realize you are an international with potentially a different point of view. That's fine. It's a compliment, not a pick-up. Answer their question in French if you possibly can and show your willingness for further conversation by continuing with observations on the same or a different topic.

The main topics to avoid are: a person's age, how much money they make and what they do for a living. Americans note: the very "ice-breaker" question that starts most conversations in America, "What do you do?", is strictly none-of-your-business in polite conversation in France, even at private parties among friends of friends.

In the beginning, the less said about your personal life or theirs, the better. So, what are you going to talk about? The French are well-informed about world politics, history and the arts. They will have opinions and they will be interested in hearing yours.

Your most important preparation as a conversationalist, besides learning the language itself, will be a willingness to analyze world politics, art and culture. Be interesting, be amusing, be yourself. The more you know about French aspects of these topics, the better, of course. (We have recommended reading at the back of the book to help you get started.)

But even general questions like "How do you feel about the Channel Tunnel?" are perfectly acceptable to break the ice with a stranger. Don't be afraid to criticize things you feel strongly about, but be ready to distinguish between something you don't understand and something you can argue clearly.

My interest in conversation is learning something, not arguing my point. So I can bat ideas back and forth all day. Arguing in France is not proselytizing!

You will have made general opinions about the French from the contacts you have had. That's fine. You will also hear plenty of criticism of the French from other internationals. The important thing is not to get "stuck" in your ideas. Be willing to accept new reasons for old observations. Studying culture, your own or anyone else's, takes a perpetually open mind.

Cultural stereotypes are something each of us strives to rise above, as individuals. The French may complain about "the French" because they each see themselves as individuals, first. Your job is to understand the valid reasons underlying the seemingly "unreasonable" behavior of the French! (Hint: There are usually more than one.)

Use each conversation with a stranger as a chance to learn something more.

Speak Softly

Whatever you talk about, remember to moderate your voice! Talking at normal volume in a shop or restaurant with friends, the *patron* or anybody else, will disturb others and will be considered very rude.

In a small French restaurant, where the tables are squeezed tightly together, anything approaching normal volume is too loud. The French love to talk, but they are extremely courteous of other people's desire to do so in public places. Speak as though no one but your interlocutor should be aware you are speaking.

We have all been embarrassed by our fellow countrymen speaking too loudly, especially if they are in a large group. We are all guilty of this. Having one or more of your own countrymen along with you anywhere puts you into a little cultural "bubble" of your own. Suddenly, the rules of your own society apply, not those of the culture around you.

Groups of tourists are conspicuous and usually unattractive everywhere because of the cultural insulation their numbers provide. Try to remember that the French speak very softly in public places, much lower than they would at home, as a consideration to others. Moderate your voice. That is the golden rule of conversation in France.

Conversation as a Dance or Drama

"Everything can be seen from several angles and in several lights.

—Montaigne

French conversation has elements of dance and drama. It is the major form of entertainment in France. The most popular television program in Paris for years was a literary talk show called *Apostrophe*.

Even if you find a French person who speaks English to you, you'll want to know some of the rules of French conversation. Seek topics that will interest your listener and keep your commentary lively, animated and brief. Don't turn a question into a lecture, holding the floor. It is rude to the other conversants and it threatens to bore, the worst offence you can make.

Don't take a conversation as an opportunity to unload your personal problems. Make it an amusing or horrible incident, if you must focus on your own life. And keep it short, with some point other than your own personal history to be made.

Let the focus of the conversation move around to different topics. Each person should contribute little snatches of appropriate comment, tossing the conversation back and forth, like a ball. If you are asked where you come from, expect to hear something of the other person's experiences in that place or that country.

You can reply with a question on an unrelated topic of interest, though some mental transition is usually involved. In a restaurant, you can always talk about the food (a favorite topic), the political situation somewhere in the world, some recent incident not clear to you, or that gave you an insight into the French. The mess America is making of things everywhere is usually an easy place to start, but try to create something constructive, enlightening, out of it.

In other words, THINK. And give your conversation partners the benefit of that effort!

As the ball goes back and forth, keep acknowledging the speaker, with little sighs or nods of agreement. (There is a special way the French say *Oui*, while sucking air in, that is a popular way of doing this.) Show yourself to be listening attentively. If you are getting bored, change the subject to something that is on your mind.

Raymonde Carroll likens French conversation to a spider's web. A good one is made up of many different threads and angles, creating a beautiful and complex shape at its end. It is unnecessary, in fact, undesirable, to seek a common point of view with your interlocutors. To distinguish is an intellectual aim. To remark upon similarities is not so interesting. This is less difficult for the English, accustomed to the art of debate than it is for Americans, who normally offer agreement just to be polite.

Interrupts are also perfectly acceptable in French conversation. One French conversant need only give the slightest pause for the other to cut in with his response. If you don't give a pause, your French interlocutor will probably break in. That's not being rude, that's being participatory. Be witty, be funny. The rapidity of the interruptions and the even the volume of the exchange may increase as the conversants get more excited ... like a dance that gets faster and faster.

A lively conversation is a successful interaction. As intensity builds, punctuations of loud laughter and even explosions of anger may occur. Don't be alarmed. Drama is part of the debate, and the quest is only for a better understanding of the topics covered and a deeper respect for the intelligence of the individual players involved. A frenzy of disagreement may suddenly collapse into a new subject; the pace changed, the players move on.

Such dramatic conversations can even develop with strangers. I have been involved in heated and interesting debate with people on a train or in a café. But your best chance is with French people at a table. Animated conversation happens often with friends in restaurants, or at a dinner party. Watch a few of them quietly to see how they play. The original meaning of *converser* in French was "to live with some one". There is a delicious intimacy established with good conversation. That is why the French consider it so important and make so much of it.

Silence between Friends

As conversation implies a degree of commitment to the other person, the closer you are to another person, the less silent you would expect to be in their presence. Silence between friends can imply indifference, or even hostility. Often friends will sit in a car or café together and chatter away in relatively meaningless babble. That is sometimes to prevent a silence developing between them, to keep each other "active" and "cheery". At that point, the French may seem to an outsider to talk too much about nothing. No, they are just avoiding the lonely distance silence might bring. It is a kind of mutual support system.

Conversational Confrontations with Strangers

Not every conversation with a stranger will start out as polite and friendly banter. Perhaps because it is so awkward to break through that polite barrier of silence with strangers, the French have perfected the *engueulade*, an argument. It is common in Paris, especially among the French. They will start at each other in confrontation, for no apparent reason.

Here, a negative comment serves to get the conversation started, to force the other guy to get involved. This is seen by other cultures as creating argument, but in France it is really an excuse for a dialogue. It is not always the best way to solve a problem. I've found I get much more from the French with a smile and polite request. But some people work in mysterious ways.

Early on in your life in Paris, you may find yourself in a confrontation with a stranger over some minor point: traffic protocol, the place in line in a queue … any number of small situations can flare up into a negative verbal exchange in France. When a French person

feels insulted or embarrassed, he may respond by criticizing the source of that insult.

There are several reasons this is often acceptable behavior. First, any recognition of a stranger is a step towards acceptance. The mere fact the person is taking off his public mask of indifference to get into conversation establishes a concern, almost a form of intimacy, with you. Criticism is more acceptable in France because it allows the other person to then give his point of view. Thus, a healthy airing of opinion can be established. Criticizing is not the same as insulting.

International journalist Stephen O'Shea gives an hilarious view of the way this unique Parisian attitude is misunderstood:

"Foreigners put out by this [rude] behavior lack sophistication, for they have not realized that showing discourtesy is a Parisian way of paying a compliment. They know nothing of Paris' *code incivil*, the Gallic equivalent of Miss Manners, and its golden rule: the ruder you are to people, the greater value you give to their existence. Thus, Parisians who respect you will shower you with pleasant little incivilities from time to time – but only after you've shown yourself worthy of insult. To attain this status, you must master the art of pointless quarrel, the *engueulade*. Arguing is to the modern Frenchman what thinking was to Descartes, a proof of existence. *Vitupero ergo sum*, I bicker, therefore I am. And the better you bicker the bigger you are."

In the section on "Getting Respect" we will discuss how to play the put-down game. For now, there are two more important points to make about the *engueulade*:

Being the Child

If the person giving the criticism is decidedly older than the receiver, there may well be a parent/child relationship at work here. It is even more a compliment, in this case! Parents criticize their children in the process of bringing them up properly. By criticizing other young people, they are thereby taking responsibility for them, breaking the mask of indifference to play a parent role and help guide the younger person along.

In this case, discussion is not so much expected on your part as a display of appreciation for the older person's concern! Argument is a game in France and criticism can be a positive, personal contribution. Take your lumps gracefully. Show you are *bien élevé* (well-raised). Accept the criticism and thank the speaker for his concern!

Being at Fault

There is one thing French people do not usually want to be at, that is, wrong. They don't mind being mistaken, being educated and becoming better informed. But they don't like to be at fault. My first reaction is usually to accept the fault, if something goes wrong. You don't necessarily need to do that. But never lay the blame specifically upon someone else in France. You will just get an uncooperative and hostile French person on your hands. You don't need to take the fault, just don't deliver the blame. Seek solutions to the problems. Which is what conversation is all about!

NO, THE FRENCH DO NOT SPEAK ENGLISH

"In another language, you not only say things differently,
you say different things."
—Joseph Barry, *The People of Paris*

So many cultured, civilized things about France to enjoy, yet the French are not easy to understand. Few of them are comfortable speaking English. They discuss things endlessly among themselves in French and they jump around from topic to topic a lot. Though they don't always look particularly happy as they converse, they obviously do it a lot.

You miss a great deal, not speaking French in France. Criticism is a way of getting to the heart of the matter here, and nothing of significance happens without lengthy discussion and deliberation ... in French.

The biggest single reason people have negative experiences in France is because they will not or cannot speak the language. Speaking French, at any level, will be enormously helpful to you in gaining respect and support among the French.

Muster up your linguistic courage and plunge in. Your bad grammar and poor vocabulary will be forgiven more readily than none at all. Paris entertains more first-time, ill-prepared travelers than any other city on earth and it is a tribute to the true humanitarian spirit of Parisians that so many confused, dumb, rude, loud and lost souls are accommodated. The least you can do is try to speak their language.

Chauvinism is a French word, taken from the fictitious but typical soldier of Napoleon, M. Chauvin, who didn't understand anything but soldierly devotion to his leader. French loyalties die slowly, and so they are not consistent. There is still a begrudging respect for the titled classes, for the Church and for the principles of equality.

While the world speaks English now as the international language of business, the French still feel theirs is the international language of culture and of refinement. They love their language and their literature and they have all studied it thoroughly in school.

While you will not be expected, as a mere foreigner, to speak French well, you will be encouraged, from the first word, to try more. And you will be complimented for your efforts.

Start with simple things: the numbers, polite phrases, and the spelling of your name in the French alphabet. Polly Platt has Ten Magic Words she recommends as the most important in the language: *Excusez-moi de vous déranger, Monsieur (Madame), mais j'ai une problème* ... ("Excuse me for bothering you, Sir, but I have a problem.") That gets the French every time. Under that cool reserve, they really want to help.

Speaking and Thinking in French

As you get to know the language better, you will soon find a separate reality to the French language. It is not just a way of speaking, but also a way of thinking. Although sociologists and linguists differ in their opinions about the effects of language on one's perception of reality, French is certainly the best key to the French mind. Many comparisons between English and French reflect basic differences in the Gallic and Anglo-Saxon approaches to life. Whole books have been written on the subject, so we'll just mention a few of them and refer you to further reading in the back.

The most obvious difference is that French, like other European languages, includes a sexual element missing in English. All French nouns are either masculine or feminine and the articles and adjectives must agree. Is it the language that makes the French so conscious of sex in their lives or the other way around? Who knows, but learning the gender of French nouns will keep the differences more firmly in your mind.

Another characteristic always uppermost in French is the relationship between the speakers. Like the Japanese, the French reserve certain forms of address for certain relationships. Luckily, there are only two different forms of addressing a person in French.

The second person singular, *tu/toi*, is reserved for close friends and family members of the same age or younger. The more formal second person form, *vous*, and its agreeing verb forms are used otherwise. Even in the more informal society of today, *vous* is used by hip teenagers speaking to adults. The formality of the way a person is addressed is important.

Madame or *Monsieur* and a person's title, such as *Monsieur le directeur*, are used to address a business associate who is your superior. Until you know a person well, use their last name to address them, along with *Monsieur*, *Madame* or *Mademoiselle* and the *vous* forms, of course.

Mademoiselle is used with girls too young to be reasonably married (Mademoiselle Chanel was an exception). As you become better acquainted, your French friends and colleagues will ask you to switch to first names, but they will expect you to continue with *vous*.

Only much later, when friendships are really established, should you begin using the *tu/toi* and never with your elders or superiors. You can imagine how this language distinction regiments relationships. We will cover this subject in greater detail in the section on making friends.

French is also a more nominal language, while English is more verbal. That means that nouns in French are more important. Nouns categorize things, an important aspect of French thinking and planning. Verbs are more important in English because action is so primary to Anglo-Saxon thinking. Direction of action is secondary.

The Frenchman will often devise an intricate *Grand Plan* before he takes any action, as you will learn in the section on art and architecture. The star patterns of the roads of France mean you don't want to start off on the wrong foot. It may take our French speaker a great deal of ruminating, including many meetings with colleagues, to devise his plan. Talking it all out with everyone first, considering every possibility, will be required before action is taken.

When a Frenchman does take action, usually his goal is set. Consequently, the direction of the action is usually built into French verbs. In English, it tends to be tacked on as an adverb or preposition. In English, for example, he goes down or up the stairs, in French, *il descend l'escalier* or *il monte l'escalier*. In French your direction is built into the action, so you have to know exactly where you are going before you start.

There are many little differences like this that help make the French understandable as you learn the language. But don't overlook the beauty of the language itself! If you take an intensive course in French before you arrive, don't be discouraged if speaking seems different than it was in the classroom. You have to pick up the way the French speak it, the musicality of language. Once you are in France, listen to the people around you. Imitate them. Use their inflections and tones. You'll soon get it.

Faux Amis

There are certain words you will learn that are false-friends in French. They do not mean the same thing in French and English, although they look the same. Here are a few of them:

adorer	to adore (in French is only the third degree of "to like")
aimer	to love (in French really means "to like")
detester	to detest (really means to "dislike")
brésilien	transsexual
car	bus (not automobile)

composter	to validate a ticket
correspondance	to change train lines (also has the English meaning)
dame âgée	older woman (a term of respect in French)
demander	to ask (not "to demand")
location	to rent
sortie	exit

No matter how good you get, a major stumbling block with Parisian French is the *argot* or slang words that young people are thinking up all the time. Even the books on the subject quickly become obsolete. Start spending time with teenagers. That's the best way to learn "in" (*branché*) French.

LEARNING FRENCH

In French, to learn and to teach are rendered by the same verb, *apprendre*. Children know this instinctively and they have little trouble with either. Though we cannot say learning French is painless, much work has been done on teaching methods. Summarizing a lifetime in language and linguistics, John Dennis, professor at San Francisco State University, here summarizes his approach to language learning as it relates to French. He gives hope and help to those who find it difficult to learn French.

Au Secours! (Help!)

In a well-known American film, a young, cheerful student of about 19 has failed his entrance examinations into a prestigious American university. His exasperated father hires an outrageously attractive woman to tutor him, her payment based on his passing the exam. The subject at hand? French grammar.

In the occasional scenes where anything remotely academic occurs, we see the young man stumbling through the present tense of *être*, the verb "to be": "Zhuh swee, too (um) ess, ill (ah) ess – est – et? ell est …"

His pronunciation is appalling, but never mind, we admire his progress ... both with French and with the tutor, as romance springs between them and becomes the major part of the film, implying that pillow talk is perhaps the best way to develop a language skill. In the end, the young man passes his exam, the tutor is rewarded handsomely and the viewer is left with a variety of misconceptions about the French language and learning a foreign language, in general.

Excusez-moi ... (Excuse me ...)

Here are the various messages that the film presented:
1. French is an inherently difficult language.
2. French grammar is more complex than the grammar of other languages.
3. Success in learning to speak French depends basically on mastery of French grammar.
4. French pronunciation presents problems because the French language has more sounds than other languages have.
5. The methodology of teaching French as a foreign language depends basically on the ability of non-native speakers to memorize and to reproduce exactly.
6. Native speakers of French tend to speak so rapidly that foreigners can't understand them.
7. French is the language of love/diplomacy/logic.

All these ideas are wrong. The only truth about the film was: pillow talk is one way to learn to communicate in any language. If that is not among your options ...

Ecoutez-moi (Listen up)

A great deal of your success or failure in learning a foreign language depends on your attitude towards the language and the capabilities you assume for yourself, as a language learner. Let's try to set things straight. To put it simply, either you take charge of yourself and the language you intend to learn, or it takes charge of you, which means you are overwhelmed and fall back on the excuses exposed above. As adults, we don't have the opportunities that we had as children when we acquired a native language. For the first three years of our lives, learning a language was our major activity. Learning another language, later on, is quite a different experience.

When we learned our mother tongue, we had no options. With a new language, we have to have a motive, an answer to the question, "Why do I have to do this?" The answers vary, but one thing is clear: it is most unlikely that the language you begin as an adult will ever approach the dimensions of your native language. This should relieve some of your anxiety and help to simplify your task. Some other words of support:

1. No language is inherently difficult. Languages are more or less difficult as foreign languages, depending on the native language(s) of the learner.
2. The same applies to grammar.
3. Learning to speak a foreign language depends primarily on one's desire to speak, then on one's need to say certain things, on one's ability to imitate new or modified sounds with accuracy, and on one's choice of vocabulary and structures to present the messages. To put grammar first, is to confuse the grammar of a language – it's anatomy, so to speak – with the language itself, which consists of more than grammar (as a person is more than his anatomy).
4. The other four ideas on the previous page are *bêtise*, either patently untrue or unsound judgements. Subscribing to any of them will inhibit your ability to learn any language.

Montrez-moi (Show me)

Without attempting a substantial analysis of the distinctive features of the French language, we can point to certain things that make French seem strange and difficult to learners of French as a foreign language.

The sound system of French contains 15 vowels, four of which are nasalized, produced through the nose instead of through the mouth.

Of the remaining 11 vowels, three are uncommon in other languages. The "r" sound in French is a distinctive "scrape" and takes a good deal of practice to reproduce accurately.

There is a way of connecting words through linking the last sound of one to the first sound of another: Il est-t-arrivé.

There is a practice of stressing the final syllable of words in French: incroyABLE instead of inCREDible. And for the literate learner of spoken French, there are more than a few instances of silent letters: *homme, sable, fort, sous, tabac, difficile*. These silences occur in the beginning, middle and end of the words.

The two most common problems cited by learners are these:
- Gender – the use of the articles *la, le, l'* and *une, un*.
- Complements of verbs – the use of prepositions after verbs: *venir à* or *de, décider à* or *de, promettre à* or *de*.

Verb tense, aspect and mood are also somewhat mystifying, especially the subjunctive. Vocabulary can be easily sorted out into a list determined by frequency of use, which ranges from high-frequency words such as articles, prepositions and pronouns, to the generic verbs (come, go, wait, buy, think, see, etc.), the generic nouns (numbers, house, market, bread, fruit, meat, etc.) and attributes (left, right, large, small, good, bad, expensive, cheap, etc.)

Learning appropriate cultural behavior (manners, etiquette, po liteness) is less likely to be integrated into language learning outside the country where it is spoken. However, when learning French in a country where French is spoken, you have the advantage of cultural behavior, as well. The relationship between what one says and how one says it (intonation of speech and body gesture), where and when one can say it, all should be integrated into any language learning experience. The culture needs to be learned and understood along with the language.

It is probable and desirable that learners will understand more language than they will produce, and that they will learn things they may not be able to say in polite society, and that certain practices and conventions will puzzle them and confuse them. Such matters are normally found in the course of learning the ways of life of a new language and culture.

Apprenez! (Learn! Teach Yourself!)

The list of possible obstacles to the learner of French is neither lengthy nor formidable. The French verb *apprendre* can mean both learn and teach. This is not ambiguous but complementary: teaching and learning are two sides of the same coin. Children know this, without being able to tell us how they know it or what they know. The learning strategies used by children in the first language are both instructive and useful to older learners who are teaching themselves and being taught.

For pronunciation, you will need an excellent model, preferably a native speaker. Not only must your pronunciation be intelligible, it must be accurate 95% of the time! For grammar and vocabulary, you can be comforted by these figures: you can get by with 50% accuracy in grammar and you can get by with a general vocabulary that comprises 5% of the high frequency words used by native speakers!

Attending classes is the most common way that people learn foreign languages. Classes are structured; they are generally taught by qualified instructors; they are relatively inexpensive; they provide a social setting for the communicative function of language.

And yet, when you ask people how they learned to speak and understand (and perhaps to read and write) a foreign language, the number who learned it in school, in language classes meeting three to five hours a week, is a distinct minority. Most people have other ways of learning, some formal, some informal.

When we say "learn" we need to understand the implications of that word. You can "learn" French sufficiently to survive: to eat, find a hotel room, find the toilet, find the *métro*, add up the restaurant bill, and so on. This kind of learning is "*primi* (from *primitif*) *Français*". You should be able to learn this type of French fairly quickly, since you are going to ignore 50% of the grammar, acquire only the vocabulary you need and practice your pronunciation. *Primi Français* is limited but functional.

A step above and beyond that is mini-French, which uses articles and conjugates verbs and adds attributes. It is the French of French children who are learning their language. It contains a considerably larger vocabulary and attempts to observe the speech contours of French statements and questions instead of the hortatory, declamatory production of primi French. Thus one moves from from *Pain, s'il vous plaît* to *Je voudrais du pain, s'il vous plaît.*

A tutor who is a native speaker of a foreign language may prove to be a good solution for learners who have gone beyond the practices of the classroom and want to create their own programs. Tutors may be expensive, so you should have fairly compelling reasons for giving up the classroom or self-instruction with good tapes and texts. Tutors who are simply agreeable native speakers will probably not have sufficient experience or skill to satisfy the learner looking for alternative ways of learning.

As television, video tapes, video disks and computers show us the potentialities for language instruction, we may find that public programs and private tutors (for small groups and individuals) will become a dominant mode of learning foreign languages. However, it is too early to tell.

Envoi (The Moral of the Story)

Learning French may not be necessary for people who want to visit for a short time in France. The French are beginning to speak English on a broader basis, in part because of their hopes for a European community. The common language of trade will be English. However, nationalities and languages will be retained and one may very well imagine primi-English and mini-English spoken from the Benelux countries to Greece. *Plus ça change, plus c'est la même chose ...*

Chapter Four

FRENCH CULTURE AND SOCIETY

THE VISUAL ARTS AND THE FRENCH PSYCHE
The Circles of French Life

The art and architecture in any culture say a great deal about what people value and how they relate to each other and to the world. One of the first things visitors notice about France is the unique radiating star patterns in the layout of the cities, especially if they try to drive around one of them.

The whole country is organized in these circles. Some would say French people think in circles, and to some extent, they do. They live in circles, and the circles of their lives link to each other, so family, work, art, food, music, sex and architecture all connect.

The supreme example in Paris architecture is the circle around the Arc de Triomphe, what is affectionately known as the Etoile, or the Star. From a dozen streets you can get a view of the Arc de Triomphe. Once you reach the Arc, however, you then face half a dozen lanes of traffic going around it, each vehicle seeking its preferred of these 12 exits.

If you were not intimidated by French ways by now, this will do it. If you don't know where you are going before you enter the Etoile, you may never get out. To understand the Gallic mind, you must think in these interconnected star patterns. From pre-Roman times, French roads have formed a mosaic of interlocking circles, with large towns in the center, surrounded by market villages, each a center for the hamlets clustered around it. Although the Romans attempted to divide Gaul into three parts, you can still see this Gallic star pattern in any road map.

The biggest star of all in France is formed by the 20 major highways leading in and out of Paris in one giant star, although the modern Périphérique leads traffic around the outside of the city now, as well as into the city's own circular centers.

These circles link a country of wide regional diversity (as will be discussed in the section on "Cuisine and Character by Region") in a unique way. Edward T. Hall in his book *The Hidden Dimension* talks about the sociopetal or socially-centered aspects of the French. They connect all points and all functions to center points, in geography, in society and in business.

"It is incredible how many facets of French life the radiating star pattern touches," Hall says. "It is almost as though the whole culture were set up on a model in which power, influence and control flowed in and out from a series of interlocking centers."

French life revolves around social relations in "a series of radiating networks". In a French office, for example, the manager's desk will often be in the middle of the room. He or she is the central figure in a hierarchy that involves many equals working as satellites around a common manager. Rather than a patriarchal pyramid, with all power focused at the top, France can been seen as "a series of radiating networks that build up into a larger and larger center".

The only problem with this sort of organization is that it demands you start out in the right direction in the first place, otherwise you get progressively off base. The wrong turn off the Etoile, for example, will lead you further and further from your goal. In a proper grid pattern, like the ancient planned city of Xian, China, you have many ways to reach a destination, all equally workable.

Thus, before taking any steps, a French person is likely to want a great deal of discussion and consideration of the options available. He will be very concerned about the goal towards which he is going and the correct plan for getting there, before he takes his first step. A good Anglo-Saxon or Chinese, on the other hand, will charge right out towards a goal, figuring he can amend his ways as he goes along.

This emphasis on goals among the Gauls is illustrated in other aspects of French life, including the language and politics. French architecture also illustrates the French sense of themselves. Visit Versailles to get a feeling for the power, the richness of what was the culmination of French monarchy. The splendor of this former France lives on in each French heart, even though France is no longer the center of world power politics. Everyone knows the history.

The 16th Century

In the 16th century, the Renaissance came to France from Italy. The discovery of the rest of the world, the rediscovery and development of the sciences and the development of the printing press in Germany all created an intellectual explosion across Europe.

Everything was questioned, including God, and later, the monarchy. King François I invited Italian artists of the day to France. Leonardo da Vinci (who actually died in France), Benvenuto Cellini and Titian decorated his new castle at Fontainebleau so magnificently that other wealthy landowners took up the trend. The chateaux of the Loire valley remain in evidence. In 1546, the new Louvre castle and the Tuileries were begun in Paris, built upon the foundations of city fortifications going back to Roman times.

In the 17th century, Paris became the great capital city of Europe. Under the direction of Cardinal Richelieu, the streets were paved and the Ile St. Louis and Marais filled with magnificent *hôtels*, the city homes of the wealthy, both aristocrats and the new merchant class.

The Luxembourg palace and gardens were completed on the left bank, the Louvre enlarged and gilded. Simon Vouet, the painter of the day, was followed by his pupils, Le Sueur, Mignard and Charles Lebrun, who did the portraits of the great families during the reign of Louis XIV, the apogee of the French monarchy.

It was this King Louis who built Versailles into a magnificent central point of royal power – economically, socially and physically. Here, he kept his nobles in splendid confinement, encouraging their petty infighting and squabbles to prevent their gathering force against him. American presidents could well learn this technique when dealing with Congress.

Although the French people ultimately rebelled against this centralization of wealth and power, these palaces remain the visible foundations of French identity, even as they romance the simple life.

In the poor countryside of the 17th century, artists such as Georges de la Tour and the brothers Lenain depicted the simple peasant and his work. That humanism became the foundation of the democratic principles that function today and is symbolized by the young, bare-chested peasant woman on the paper money and the stamps of France. Fondly known as "Marianne", she has represented the French since the French Revolution, although a working alternative to the monarchy took 100 years to achieve.

The turbulent politics of the 18th century brought a decline in the decorative arts. Philosophy predominated. Art and architecture became a function of political thinking. The Bastille prison was torn down and its stones used in the bridge built at the Place de la Concorde. The people could then walk on this symbol of oppression as they crossed the Seine to the steps of the Assemblée Nationale, one of the bicameral legislative bodies that today sets laws according to the will of the people. The other, the Sénat, is next to the Jardin de Luxembourg.

The 19th Century

Napoleon came to power in 1799 with the monarchy his model. He also censored art and literature but encouraged public architecture. In the middle of the 19th century, Napoleon's nephew, Louis Napoleon Bonaparte, declared he wanted to be a second Augustus Caesar and make Paris a second Rome. He named Baron Georges Haussmann, the prefect of the Seine, to create the Paris we see today. Other cities in France and then elsewhere in the world have followed his basic design elements: wide, tree-lined boulevards, underground sewer systems and centralized water supplies, large parks, standardized heights of buildings and density limitations. Much of the old haphazard Paris was torn down to create this new one. Controversial at the time, Haussmann's ideas had the approval and support of an autocrat. He transformed the city in only 20 years.

Parisians now relish their city, their parks and the remarkable architecture that is Haussmann's carefully protected legacy. Thanks to good planning and some good luck, the city of Paris remains a great work of art in itself.

The visual arts began to flourish in France once again in the second half of the 19th century. There were three schools: the romantic painters such as Delacroix and Gericault, the realists, Ingres and Courbet and the symbolism of Corot, which lead to Impressionism.

Monet and Renoir led this new artistic movement, a brave force against the art establishment of the day. Art historians credit the sunlit ripples of the painting *The Seine at La Grenouillère* as the first

Impressionist painting, done in 1869. These two artists developed the full style. Camille Pissarro, Degas and Cézanne soon joined them. The next generation included Georges Seurat and Paul Gauguin. The value of the individual impression, however, has remained an essential element of art to this day.

The 20th Century

France continued to be a center for individual artistic expression in the 20th century, drawing the likes of Henri Matisse, Pablo Picasso (Spanish, but adopted by the French), Paul Klee (Swiss-German) and Georges Braque.

Museums and galleries, many of them the refurbished *hôtels* (private homes) of the 16th and 17th century, sprung up all over Paris. While artists and writers were supposed to starve romantically in Paris garrets, art itself became the domain of the wealthy elite. Nothing, save eating, sex and politics, is more sacred to the French middle-class sensibility. A person who cares nothing for art is considered uncivilized in France, no matter how rich or successful he may otherwise be.

Artists and writers today still enjoy the time-honored status of visionaries, impoverished and angry outsiders though they be. Visit an art exposition in Paris, especially an opening vernissage, to get a sense of this. Being beautifully dressed and participating in the local art scene, whether it is painting, fashion or film, are basic ingredients of being refined in France.

Behind this superficial cultural propaganda is a profound appreciation of life, of living, as an art form. Paris is a work of art, but so are the circles of life in France. Everything is connected and everyone is aware of that. Everything is important, from architecture to literature to personal dress; all must reflect that dynamic, sensual aesthetic that gives value to life. Money? Only a rather coarse means to a far more important end, and not the only path to that goal, at all.

POLITICS AND SOCIETY

"… the French seem to abound in contradictions and are not overly disturbed by it. They profess lofty ideals of fraternity and equality, but at times show characteristics of utmost individualism and selfish materialism. They seem restless, hypercritical of their government and capitalism, yet they are basically conservative."

—Robert T. Moran

Four centuries of literature and philosophy provide ample evidence of the French love of politics and concepts such as the uniqueness of the individual and the right of self-determination. While the notion of democracy was not invented in France, its principles are fiercely defended there, although the French argue continually among themselves about how that should be accomplished. The range of French political philosophies covers a wide spectrum, helped along by a love of analytical thinking that is the bedrock of the education system and a free and inquiring press.

There is nothing that the French love to read about and talk about so much as politics and philosophy. France's heroes are its political and literary figures, not its rock stars. (Mussolini and Hitler agreed once that France was ruined by alcohol, syphilis and journalism.)

"How bored we would be," Chateaubriand is credited with saying, "if it were not for politics."

The minute you move among the French, you are engaged in political discussion. Your cab driver will rail against the current government, the gentleman at the next table at a café will blame the communists and the student in your train compartment will condemn the bourgeois establishment. Everyone will expect you to have an opinion, too.

Whether or not you speak French, you'll be diving right into politics, yours, France's and everyone else's. It will help you to know something about recent political history here.

A Little Recent History

You do not need to remind the French that the main reason they still have their beautiful Paris and the magnificent castles and cathedrals scattered across the country is because they were forced to surrender to the Nazis early in World War II. The Allied victory brought France her freedom, but the dismal first half of the century had left her economically and politically in shambles.

War hero Charles de Gaulle was made premier of a provisional government and then in 1946, the Fourth Republic was formed and the post-war industrialization of France began, but the political structure proved unstable, time and again. There were 22 govern-ments in 12 years.

Finally, in 1958, de Gaulle led a coup, establishing the Fifth Republic, which gave greater constitutional powers to the president and thus stability to the system. In spite of a bitter war in Algeria, he remained popular and the economy revived.

France still functions under this Fifth Republic, with echoes of the monarchy which ended 200 years ago. The president lives in the 18th century Elysée palace, home of Madame de Pompadour, two Napoleons and the official residence of the presidents of France since 1873. Social class distinction maintains a fairly unchanged though rela-tively impoverished titled class.

The Communist party in France grew strong in the first decade after the war and leftist ideas were popular in the 1960s, both with students and the working-class unions, leading to major riots in 1968. The country's leadership, however, remained under "rightist", or capitalist, control. The presidency passed from de Gaulle to Georges Pompidou to Valérie Giscard d'Estaing.

Then, François Mitterrand, a Socialist, won the election in 1981 by just 51% as the right split its votes between the parties of Giscard and Jacques Chirac. (On his third try, 14 years later, Chirac finally became the President.) It was the first time since 1936 that a coalition of centrists, socialists and communists had won a presidential election and there were parties on the streets of Paris all night, reflecting the spirit of the storming of the Bastille nearly two centuries earlier which began the French Revolution.

Everybody expected big changes in government policy. Some changes came. Mitterrand dissolved the National Assembly and called an election. The result was a socialist landslide. Over half of those newly elected were from the teaching profession, a traditional source of liberal, anti-capitalist thinking.

Not everybody celebrated Mitterrand's victory, however. The stock market froze as the players panicked the morning after the

National Assembly election. Investors' money poured out of France. Mitterrand maintained the value of the franc for as long as possible, hoping confidence would resume, and began fulfilling his election promises: five weeks of paid vacation, a 10% increase in salaries and optional retirement at 60 were among the first new laws passed. These new rights covered every worker in the country.

In 1982 Mitterrand nationalized much of the public service sector, including many banks, fuel and power suppliers, steel factories, and some electronics, chemical and telecommunication firms. (Many aspects of French industry, particularly banking, had been in the hands of government since World War II, in spite of capitalist leadership.)

The new Auroux laws strengthened the powers of the unions in the nationalized companies, giving the workers more control than they had ever known before. At that time, about 20% of the voters in France still considered themselves communists. About 30% of the workforce were in government jobs. Today it is closer to 40%.

None of Mitterrand's moves changed the basic power structure of France, however. In government, especially, the Ecole Nationale d'Administration (the ENA, whose graduates are called *énarques*) which was created by de Gaulle to train top administrators, produces most of the political figures of France today. Although admission to this school is by very competitive examination, the bias is somewhat in favor of the children of the educated classes.

The "other" school which breeds France's leaders, on the business side, is the Ecole Polytechnique or "X", founded by Napoleon as a military training school in 1804. Many of the graduates of both schools go into the private sector, keeping their former classmates as close political friends. So, in spite of the new government leadership, the running of both the government and of the nationalized companies remained in basically the same hands.

Up to 1985, the European economy was in crisis and the French franc was falling in value. By 1985 it took more than ten francs to buy a US dollar. People began to lose faith in the changes the Socialists could affect.

In the next parliamentary election, 1986, the right returned to power in the Assembly and Mitterrand was forced to "cohabit" as President with rightist Jacques Chirac as Prime Minister. Chirac (an *énarque*) was already the first Mayor of Paris (The first because Paris had always been run by the 20 *arrondissement* mayors, before this new post was created.)

A pupil of Georges Pompidou and a man on the right (the RPR), Chirac quickly privatized a number of state-run organizations and the force of the socialist movement seemed doomed. But Mitterrand enjoyed a revenge in the 1988 presidential election, regaining both his Presidency (he serves a seven-year term) and a majority in the Assembly, though he had to join forces with the communists to do so.

With a majority in the Assembly, Mitterrand could then choose another socialist (and *énarque*), Michel Rocard, as his prime minister. Rocard stopped the privatization programs and attempted a more leftist balance among the various political forces.

In local elections of 1989, the country started to turn conservative again and many of those left of center were booted out. Minority groups such as the French of Arabic origins found their voices and it was considered an election for the person, not for the party. The communists now could claim less than 10% of the electorate, the lowest proportion since World War II, and less than the ultra-right wing, anti-European National Front of Jean-Marie Le Pen.

Jacques Chirac was re-elected mayor of Paris for another six-year term and the issue of European Union, with the "one market" plan looming in 1992, became pre-eminent in everyone's mind. The concept of a united Europe, which was born in France, was getting little nourishment from French farmers already hurt by GATT trade agreements and French workers in a world economic recession saw an increasing number of foreign-born French taking their jobs. The Maastricht Treaty only passed in France by 51% of the vote.

The French public keeps up with political trends with the help of numerous newspapers and magazines.

In May 1993, a successful alliance of the center-right brought the RPR and the UDF together for 80% of the seats in the 577-seat National Assembly. The Socialists and their allies had only 70. It was the biggest victory sweep in France's democratic history, according to *The Economist*.

President Mitterrand, whose replacement was inevitable in elections in 1995, chose neo-Gaullist and Chirac advisor Edouard Balladur as the new Prime Minister. Balladur is also, you guessed it, an *énarque*.

In March 1994, one in four youngsters in France was out of work and 10% of the work force overall. With the legal minimum wage a generous FF5,886 a month, Balladur decided to reduce these wages by 20% for young workers entering the work force. Rather than encourage more employment, it brought the most violent student protests in France since 1968.

Taking to the streets in organized demonstrations is an important part of French life for all groups and all parties. The French love to demonstrate their political opinions, individually and in groups. You might get a transportation union strike like the one day shutdown in October 1995 which paralyzed the country, or farmers blocking the highways protesting GATT accords, or parents lobbying for better education for their children.

While calls for decentralization of government has brought more power to the local mayors' offices around the country, they still tend to come from the same source (ENA) in a kind of musical chairs of personalities of the left and the right. Respect for training and experience still runs strong with the French, even though they must get bored with the same old faces.

In 1995, with a wide range of minority candidates splitting the vote, Jacques Chirac finally slipped through as President of France over Socialist rival Lionel Jospin. Chirac won only 52.6% of the vote, but the right also won most of the regional councils and 80% of the seats in Parliament, so the mandate was clear, if not the man.

Chirac choose Alain Juppé as his Prime Minister, an *énarque* who graduated fifth in his class and is nicknamed "Amstrad" for his fast, computer-like mind. The summer following the election, Juppé was involved in a personal scandal (not involving sex, of course, this is France, but the discounted rent of the apartment of his son) and Chirac himself took enormous heat for following through on a series of nuclear bomb tests in the Pacific.

The 2002 presidential election ended with a highly publicized face off between incumbent president, Jacques Chirac, and extreme-right *Front National* (FN) founder Jean-Marie Le Pen. Le Pen's success in the first round of elections – he defeated the heavily favored socialist candidate and former prime minister Lionel Jospin – shocked much of France, and led to a massive public outcry against the reactionary politician, who is often described as a neo-fascist.

Many French were left wondering how a man who represents such intolerance and hatred was able to achieve such popularity in a culture that prides itself in exactly the opposite. Unsurprisingly, Chirac went on to win the presidency with ease, and at the same time led his newly formed conservative coalition (UMP) to a landslide victory over the dazed socialists in the following legislative elections.

The Political Parties

In your political discussions, it will be helpful for you to know the major political parties in France today:

- UMP (*Union pour un Mouvement Populaire*): Newly formed conservative coalition consisting of the former RPR, UDF, and DL parties, led by Alain Juppé.
- PS (Socialist Party): United by Mitterrand in 1971, it was the largest party in the National Assembly until the 1993 election. Its members include former prime ministers Michel Rocard and Lionel Jospin.
- PC (Communist Party): Only 9% of the voters belong to this party now, when nearly 30% of France was communist in 1946.

- FN (National Front): The right-wing organization based in Marseilles, anti-immigrant and nationalistic, and has become a major force on the French Riviera. Jean-Marie Le Pen is the leader.
- MRG (Movement of Radicals of the Left): This party maintains 8–12% of the vote, on a par with the extreme right National Front.

The legal voting age is 18 in France, and elections are always held on Sundays, with local candidates required to gain 50% of the voting total. With several different party "lists," often a runoff election must be held the subsequent Sunday to get a majority decision. In the second try, various parties will pool their votes to give one candidate a majority, so loyalties must be flexible, compromise inevitable.

STREET FASHION

"The French are full of flattery for themselves," Coco Chanel once said. Some people criticize the French, especially the Parisians, for their overwhelming concern for the way they look. Indeed, there is something of the "peacock" syndrome in Paris. People dress to show off, to display their taste and sense of class.

Tourists dressed as for a visit to Disneyland, even EuroDisney, stick out like a sore thumb in Paris, but be warned! Being well (and expensively) dressed and well-groomed can become a primary occupation. If you want to feel like you are part of the scene, take a few basic steps into fashion.

You can call it superficial, but you can't fail to admire these "peacocks". The French are not frivolous about their street clothes. Chanel herself wore her suits seven or eight years (lacking dry cleaners, she then progressed to her line of perfumes). She chose materials that would last for 20 years.

"Elegance," she said, "is the contrary of negligence." Today you will still see her little black dress, little black shoes, her classic suits and bobbed haircuts, from Paris to Hong Kong. She even instigated the fashion for a healthy tan.

The Parisians do nothing so well as dress, and it doesn't take a huge wardrobe to do it. A woman or man might own only two or three basic outfits, but each will be the best quality and fit perfectly. They will look great in them and know it. Women use scarves and jewelry to make themselves endlessly original and fresh. Men can take a single fabric, a tie, a shirt and look polished.

Paris is dressy. You won't find a professional French man or woman in jeans or running shoes here. Only tourists and maybe discount store clerks. Any French person who can manage it will dress in smart suits and dresses, every day, year around. They wouldn't dream of wearing shorts in Paris, though they calmly go nude on the beach.

One heartening thing about the French sense of fashion is that beauty knows no age. Not only is the youth syndrome less pronounced here, but the whole business of style and elegance is the domain of the experienced. "You can be irresistible at any age," Chanel said. "You have to replace youth by mystery. Elegance is the prerogative of those who have already taken possession of their future."

I find it incredible how stunning a French person can be and the trick is simply in the way they present themselves to the world. They possess a quality above and beyond the Hollywood face and body. Even young people in their required denim jeans manage to find ones that fit better and look dressier than the same uniform in other parts of the world.

After a certain age, to dress well reflects not the latest magazine trend, but taste and class. B.C.B.G. (*Bon Chic, Bon Genre*) is a term the French use for what is stylish. A great part of the drama of street life in Paris is admiring this continuously pleasant fashion spectacle. It's beyond group trendiness. It's a personal statement. We discussed some of this in the section on "Non-verbal Communication". The French don't slouch, though the young like to imitate the relaxed American look. Parisian women know how to walk with confidence, turn with style, sit and cross their legs provocatively.

The men can turn smoking a cigarette into a tantalizing gesture. Add to this physical presence and control a highly refined sense of clothing and style and you have the ingredients for a wonderful public display of fashion art. And you don't have to be young and beautiful or even thin to participate. There is beauty in each of us. The French know that and capitalize upon it.

Internationals living in Paris quickly start to pick up this fashion-and-style consciousness. I've seen women I would have pegged instantly as Perfect Parisians, only to discover as I get closer that they are speaking English with an American accent. If you appreciate the dramatic effect, you can't help emulating it.

Here are a few hints on how to start in Paris (also see the section on "Shopping"). For women: Choose dresses, suits or skirts and blouses or well-fitting pants in dark or neutral colors. Limit bright colors to one or two items: a scarf, a blouse, a sweater. Wear dress shoes, preferably dark, that are comfortable for walking. Boots are acceptable in rainy weather.

In winter, have a well-cut wool, leather or synthetic coat, dark or neutral, to go with everything and that resists rain and wind. Carry a purse big enough for your needs, which closes firmly against pick-pockets. Carry a second foldaway bag for parcels. If you must carry a backpack, get an adult-looking one and don't put anything valuable in the zip pockets. Make sure your hair is well groomed. A haircut in Paris is a good way to start.

For men: Wear good wool or corduroy pants in winter, well-cut, with a belt. Heavy wooly sweaters under your wool or leather jacket will help keep you warm in rain or wind. A "Macintosh" over everything and an umbrella will be useful. Leather moccasins or dress shoes are preferred, though more sporty shoes are acceptable now.

In the countryside, the code is less formal and on the beach, it's altogether different.

Nudity

Ironically, along with their high sense of fashion, the French also have a notorious lack of modesty. They bathe at public swimming pools and beaches in the nude. Men and women sunbathe along the banks of the Seine in summer, either nude or striped to the waist. In spite of good public toilet facilities, men will still urinate on the street.

Don't be shocked. Like the Japanese, the French don't recognize the sinful aspect of nudity, or at least hold in contempt conventional Anglo-Saxon Christian morality. Join them if you wish, but don't misinterpret such nudity as an invitation for sexual advances. You'll get a sharp rebuff. Nudity in France is another form of fashion.

FRENCH FILM: C'EST DU CINÉMA

The French have an idiom, *C'est du cinéma*, which loosely translates to: "It's all a farce," or "It's a very unlikely event." It's reassuring to know that the French distinguish between fantasy and reality, but the idiom is puzzling when one considers the significance of *le cinéma* and *les cinéastes* (film makers).

The French are absolutely gaga about *les films*. Parisians attend films at least once a week, though video rentals are decreasing that figure. Both *Pariscope* and *L'Officiel*, the competing weekly schedules for Paris films, can be found in nearly everyone's pocket. There are literally hundreds of films showing at any one time in Paris and English language films are often shown in V.O. (*version originale*) with French subtitles.

As an art, film is right up there with gastronomy in the hearts of the French. The *cinéastes* work with natural ingredients: people, places, feelings, things, colors, textures … to create a grand artifice, which the French consumer consumes as if it were as real as pastry, as tangible as life.

Picasso warned us: "All art is a lie." Two dimensions pretending to be three. *C'est du cinéma*, the idiom admonishes us. Yet we are hooked. Film is another kind of reality and there is something distinctly French about French films.

They differ in the design and strategy of their presentation, in their evident intention and in their attention to certain topics and themes. French films offer endless and wonderful insights into the French psyche and French values.

SEX AND PROSTITUTION

Sex, that is, its expression in the differences between the sexes, is a constant source of entertainment to the French and their fascination with it is apparent everywhere. Sensuality is evident in everything from architecture to shopping displays.

This is not to say that French women are loose or that free love is available. But the French love to do one thing and that they do very well. They flirt. And if you relax just a little you will find yourself enjoying the constant flirtations going on around you. You will even find yourself flirting, too.

The act of sex, for the French, is not usually the goal of the sensual game. A sexual climax in French is called *la petite mort*, or the little death, instead. Life is in celebrating the differences, not just experiencing that ultimate union.

Sex outside of marriage exists in France, as everywhere in the world, but here it is not taken as a shocking surprise or political embarrassment. "Polygamy is the opposite of monotony" goes the French saying and monotony is to be avoided at all costs, as we know from Mlle Chanel.

Marriage and the family are strong institutions in France, as defined both by the Roman Catholic Church and the Napoleonic Code. Sexual infidelity is hardly enough to cause a marriage to fall apart. Marriage in France involves many economic expectations but fewer personal ones.

Married people are friends, not joined at the hip and not necessarily with all the same interests. Mostly they share the pleasures of their children and the responsibilities to their families.

While women do not share an equal presence with men in the halls of business and politics, their presence is always appreciated and their individuality respected. You will quickly find out why if you approach a provocatively dressed French woman without proper decorum. As a woman, you can expect to be treated with respect in France and openly condemn anyone who doesn't.

Sex for Money

Prostitution was only declared illegal in 1946, just about the time that women in France finally got to vote!

Visit the Pigalle on any night of the year and you will think the world comes to Paris for sex. A wide variety of sexual tastes are promoted (and to some degree satisfied) in Paris. It is to be expected, given the general enthusiasm of the French of all things sensual.

The French don't make a particularly clear distinction between the joys of food, fashion and sex. A major resource on sex in Paris, a book called *Paris La Nuit Sexy*, devotes most of its pages to descriptions of the restaurants in town.

Certainly, if you aren't interested in prostitution, you can avoid it. But be prepared to face sensuality at every turn. The big reviews, the *Grands Spectacles* at places like the Lido, Crazy Horse Saloon, the Moulin Rouge and the Paradis Latin are designed for wowing tourist groups from Birmingham, Hokkaido and Iowa. You won't find them shocking beyond nudity. For some real titillation, you'll have to go to the erotic shows such as Théâtre des 2 Boules and Théâtre Saint-Denis or a chain of peep-shows around Paris designed for that.

Homosexuality is called "the English vice" in France, but there's lots of playing around with variations on the conventional themes here. The most discrete, anonymous way of participating in sexual games is by modem. Tap into the *Minitel*, the French computer that comes with telephone service in France.

The *Minitel*, introduced in France in the mid-80s as an electronic telephone directory, quickly became a success with "dating services" offered on-line. You can now call into the service (3615), connect your *Minitel*, then tap a code (try AC1, there are hundreds) and someone on the other side starts answering or asking questions on your screen. You can type replies as you like (there are even English language ones) because nobody knows who or what you are. Totally anonymous. Perfect for fantasizing, and you just pay via your telephone bill.

The next step up, in terms of active participation, is the erotic telephone numbers. For these you'll need a bit more French and I'm not sure how you pay.

Then there are the public bars, discotheques and dance halls. Some of these specialized: gay or lesbian sex, couples exchanges, even "S&M" (sadism and masochism) are available. So be sure you read the ads carefully and your tastes are being matched. These are usually "pick-up" places, and to do so, read the section on "Nonverbal Communication" and do the reverse of what is recommended there.

More intimate still are the clubs (*clubs de rencontres*) and the saunas which open from 10 pm to 7 am, where your participation will be expected. There are also woman "at home" you can call directly. The *Minitel* access number or the book mentioned earlier in this section will give you a directory of them. Thanks to the liberated French telephone company (run by the Government) you can let your fingers do the walking ...

Where you shouldn't walk, especially at night, is in the stunning old Bois de Boulogne, the immense woods on the western edge of Paris. This is where the weirdest action is. Fortunately for the families who would also like to enjoy this park, most of the sexual action is limited to specific areas for specific purposes at specific times. There is actually a map which indicates what kind is where. Much of the "pick-up" process and ultimately the activities themselves are done in cars, but you might avoid walking off into the woods around the Lac

Inférieur in the early evening, even in summer when it is light until 10 pm. The woods are literally littered with action.

There are many other locations for good old, straight-forward, pay-as-you go prostitution in Paris, where there are said to be 20,000 full-time prostitutes and another 60,000 working part-time. (I don't know how they conduct the census.) Basic price is 25 euros a throw (plus the hotel, if you're not in the Bois). The basic locations are fairly obvious: the train stations of Montparnasse, Gare du Nord and Gare de l'Est, the Pigalle and the Boulevard Clichy (both straight and gay), and around Les Halles.

For rock-bottom prices, try Porte de la Chapelle in the *10ème*, rue Chalon in the *12ème* and rue Houdon in the *18ème*. Higher prices and better quality can be found at the Pyramids *métro* (and nearby rue Sainte Anne for gays) and at the Avenue de la Grande Armée and Porte Maillot, not far from the Bois. Here prices jump to 50 to 75 euros. The Saint-Germain-des-Prés area in the *6ème* is mostly for gay services. Even in Paris, there are still few opportunities for straight women to buy men's services ... obviously not many paying customers.

PETS

Although a visit to any French market is convincing testimony to the love of eating all parts of all animals here, some animals, especially small dogs and cats, get better treatment than humans from the French. English writer Fay Sharman, author of *Coping with France*, is horrified by this contrast:

"The French attitude to animals is a bizarre mix of brutality, indifference and adoration. They think nothing of shooting larks and thrushes or keeping live rabbits horribly cooped up at the market ... they are altogether unsqueamish ... Yet the French have suddenly become a nation of pet lovers."

Dogs and cats bask in undeserved affection in France, especially in Paris. Owners cuddle them shamelessly. Strangers who would not

give the owner a glance will drop to their knees to give the their pet a smooch. It's a sad commentary on what is an otherwise logical group of people.

On the street, in cafés, in shops, in restaurants, nobody seems to mind a perpetually yapping miniature poodle though a human being making an equal volume would be arrested. But the most obnoxious evidence of the indulged presence of pets in Paris is the ubiquitous droppings that litter the otherwise stunning Paris sidewalks.

It is a constant complaint of visitors that you can't look up at the architecture, you're so busy looking down to avoid the dog poop. Pet owners ignore both the French "pooper-scooper" laws that require they clean up behind their animal and white dog silhouettes painted on sidewalks that remind everyone to bring Fru-fru to the curbside before allowing him to relieve himself. Pet owners and other indulgent Parisians remain tolerant of what thousands of little Totos leave behind. Yet they remark unkindly when Asian children are allowed to pee in the gutter.

Only the Mayor of Paris seems worried, spending a small fortune on all sorts of special equipment for his men in green in the sanitation department who try nobly to keep up with the problem. In addition to these sidewalk workers, other men in green with enormous trucks collect city garbage every morning, including Sundays, and city gutters are flooded with water in strict schedules to help keep the beloved City of Light clean. No matter. Pets keep the upper hand ... er, leg.

The French, whose high taxes are paying for all this clean-up, say it is actually good luck to step on dog doodoo ... a rather stoic approach to what in most urban environments is considered an avoidable nuisance. This is an inconsistency of French life few visitors can understand. The French love some small animals though they eat others; they take tremendous pride in their beautiful Paris, yet they let a poodle use it as a bathroom. What Anglo-Saxon can explain that? You will have to watch your step and walk with agility, especially in Paris, to avoid "good luck".

I had my first insight into why the French have this soft spot for pets when I became one. No, I wasn't on a leash. I was on crutches, having broken my ankle rushing too fast down the seven flights of stairs from my little *chambre de bonne* on one of my regular visits to Paris.

Believe me, Paris on crutches is a different city. People, strangers, French strangers stop to offer you assistance, to express their sympathy, to guide you across the street. Neighbors who had never acknowledged my existence in 10 years of living in the building, suddenly offered to let me access my little servant's room via their apartment's elevator. A taxi driver offered to take me to my cancelled appointment in Russia, for free. He said he'd always wanted to go, anyway.

I was incredulous, but here's how I figure it: in becoming helpless, I became like a pet, totally dependent on others for my existence. In that dependence I became worthy of far more attention and consideration than a functional person.

In the Gallic view, life is hard, cruel and ugly. It can be made to appear beautiful and pleasant and every step should be made to do so. That is why it is important to the French that things look well, regardless of the chaos and deterioration the beautiful facade might cover up. But friendliness? Hey, who are you kidding? We all know life is hard, cruel and ugly. Friendliness is reserved for those who merit the effort: the family, the friends, and the helpless.

In a hard, cruel world, little pet animals are totally dependent on us for their survival. They require our indulgence, they cannot learn to be tough, as children can; they can only beg for mercy. So it is with people on crutches. They are helpless. They deserve every indulgence. My only advice if you are on crutches in Paris: watch for the dog droppings. They are slippery.

Chapter Five

FOOD AND WINE

LE CAFÉ

"Paris is the only city I know where you have an absolute
desire to go out into the streets, to walk or to drop into a
café."

—William Gardner Smith

The café in France is something comparable to the *dim sum* teahouse
tradition of China, except smokier. Sitting for hours in the teahouse,
talking and eating *dim sum* would seem very familiar to the Frenchman, who loves nothing better than sitting, alone or with friends, in
a café, or when weather permits, outdoors on the sidewalk.

The pub scene in England also has similarities, but the bar scene in America is more distant. Talking politics and watching the world go by (both the pedestrians and the traffic) are the two favorite pastimes in a French café. It is not for pick-ups but the friendly atmosphere can quickly dispel the chill of loneliness.

Someone once said that in France they still make a distinction between the joy of accumulation and the accumulation of joys. The café is one place for the latter. I often sit for hours in a sidewalk café, with a book or postcards to write, watching the French enjoy a sunny afternoon. Otherwise, inside (trying to avoid the cigarette smoke) I can get out of the rain and snuggle up to a French newspaper or try eavesdropping on the conversations around me, without concern for the passing time.

The total cost is a single purchase of coffee: about US$1.50. The French normally drink their coffee in little cups, very strongly brewed. The *express* can be expanded by adding hot milk, called a *café crème* or watered down and served in a large cup *café américain*. No respectable café owner would consider disturbing the long, peaceful perusals of a client, even one who buys as little as a single *express*. If one more of these powerful coffees is too much, try a *citron pressé*, the freshly squeezed lemon juice to which you add sugar and water to suit your taste. Or any number of non-alcoholic *sirops*, flavored concentrates (already sugared) you dilute with water. Or the lovely herbal teas called *infusions* in many different beneficial flavors.

Since the turn of the century, the café has been an important part of social life in France. You will find the patron quite hospitable, except during the busy lunch hours. He will often engage you in conversation, once he is confident you share a common language or common interest.

Other regulars will arrive and launch into serious discussion with the patron and other friends. You get the impression that they all feel quite at home. After a few visits, you will begin to feel the same way.

It only takes a little bit of sunshine to get the French out onto the sidewalk for their café or drinks.

(See the "Conversation" section on how to get started turning the French into friends.)

You'll find exceptions to this generally friendly scene, of course, especially where cafés cater to mobs of tourists in a rush to get to the next tourist spot. In Paris, near the Opéra and American Express, or along the Champs Elysée (now mostly fast food places), and around the Louvre, the sidewalk cafés have taken on the ambiance of their non-Parisian clientele. Tourists unsure of themselves sit stunned in silence or talk loudly to their friends in languages other than French, usually about things "back home".

These places are the first retreat of the "culture shocked" and might well be avoided. The French staff can do little with such clients and go about their jobs with typical Gallic resignation, usually misinterpreted as aloofness.

Let's get back to real French cafés. These serve simple but delicious hot lunches during the business week, so during that noontime respite every table will be taken and the staff will be too busy feeding great numbers of people to worry much about hospitality.

Lunch time in Paris is fun, if a bit challenging, when you are alone. Many people eat alone, so you don't stand out. Waiters speak quickly, often too busy to give you a menu (the day's specials will be written on the chalkboard) and they never seem to make up the bill (*l'addition*) when you want it. They even confuse orders, which can be difficult to correct in the rush. But it's all part of the game.

The friendly, relaxed pace will resume after 2 pm. The best time to relax at a café is after the midday rush, when the regulars take over. Children are welcome and can even be served alcohol after the age of 14.

The food menu will not be lengthy: *un plat varié* of vegetables in season with a piece of ham, an entrecôte steak with *pommes frites*, one or two tarts for dessert. Outside of lunch time, mainly sandwiches or hot *croque-monsieurs* will be available, along with salad, ice cream and any tarts left over from lunch time.

If you are alone and want to practice your French, sit at the bar (*le zinc*, from the days when they were really made of that). Drinks will be a bit cheaper here than at a table. Once at the bar, you should stay there. If you later move to a table, the price of what you bought will go up, automatically. For whatever you order, you will be expected to pay for all you've consumed only when you leave, though the waiter may leave a little slip of paper under your plate to keep track of your *addition* as you go along.

There are several varieties on the café theme in France. They each work slightly differently, so here's a general rundown:

- *La brasserie* will be similar to a café, but larger or smarter, with a dining area featuring a wider selection of food, usually served all day. This is where to go if you are hungry at 6 pm! The same stay-as-long-as-you-like rule applies, but if you sit in the dining area, you will be expected to order a hot meal.
- *Le bar* in France is usually much smaller than a café. You pop inside for a quick drink and often stand for service. Excellent for a quick *express* and vocal political discussions but not for long, intellectual conversations. The clientele are mostly older men of working class and the conversation will usually revolve around French sports. Perfect, if you are a soccer fan.
- *Le bar à vin* has enjoyed a resurgence in popularity in France. The atmosphere is more along the lines of a café, but with wines from a specific region featured by the glass or the bottle. The food will be a plates of meats (*charcuterie*) and cheeses with fine bread to compliment the wines. Here the interest in the wines creates a particularly friendly ambiance in the best café tradition. A wine bar is also an excellent place to learn more about the nuances of the many wines regions of France. The employees will all be enthusiasts. (See the section on wines.)
- *Le salon de thé* is a more feminine and upscale version of the café. Sweet pastries and little canapés will be made and sold, usually to take away for some elegant event at home, for tea or for dessert at

a fine dinner. There will usually be a few tables where you can eat these specialties in the shop, served along with tea or an *infusion* or coffee or even an alcoholic beverage. Service usually runs all day and some expand the menu at lunch time. Conversation is rather more discrete, delivered at a lower volume. There will be no bar and little comraderie. I always imagine couples at a *salon de thé* to be clandestine lovers.

Fast food places now abound in France wherever students or tourists congregate. Even the French accept them now. Loud and impersonal, like fast food places around the world, they produce a culture shock all their own and I avoid them. But if you really need a McDonald's (*MacDo*) or a Pizza Hut, you'll easily find one.

In contracts, finding a local café and becoming a "regular" there can greatly enhance your life in France, wherever you are. The restaurateurs can also give you that "at home" feeling but are less well suited to casual conversation. For the more complex subjects of Restaurants and Cuisine, read on.

Getting Respect
"You don't have to be nice to be helpful."

—a French waitress

The person serving you in a café or a shop or any public place may be cool, at first, especially in Paris. This is often misinterpreted as indifference or hostility. It could be, but more often it is uncertainty or just professionalism.

We have already talked about the value of conversation and discussion in France. The French love to talk and especially to argue different points of view. This is an important part of social exchange. A common approach to public dialogue in France is the *engueulade* or bickering.

Not really argument, it starts with a cool, neutral "show me" approach. It is often used to establish the intentions and abilities of

both customer and client, and can lead to mutual respect and trust, handled properly.

I've seen an hour's conversation in a bicycle shop on the merits of two different bicycle tires. It was very serious and they seemed to bicker about the silliest details about each tire. As I was waiting for the shopkeeper to finish, I had to listen to this and I became a bit exasperated, but I waited my turn patiently as I knew I must.

Finally, the tire was chosen, purchased and my turn came. The shopkeeper, an Englishman who has lived in France a long time, apologised for keeping me waiting. Then I couldn't help questioning out loud the practicality of taking such a length of time to sell a single tire.

"Yes," he agreed, a little tired himself, "but I wouldn't want him to buy without considering all the options."

That's it in a nutshell.

A good French shopkeeper, clerk or waiter expects you to consider all of the options and he is there to assist you in doing it. First though, you have to convince him you really want his expertise and assistance.

A good waiter considers himself a professional. He is proud of the food he offers you, the place where he works and the food he serves. He wants your appreciation, but he wouldn't dream of putting on a Happy Face to get it. To a French person, that would be considered very insincere. (Now, in all fairness, there are times when very rushed restaurant workers and disgruntled shop clerks will not be helpful, no matter what you do, but in general, the following approach works.)

Menus in France are confusing, as we have said, even to the French. Part of every respectable waiter's job is to explain that menu. He wants you to consider all the choices and he will be your guide, but only if you ask him. When he comes to take your order, smile, establish eye contact, excuse yourself (you should have said *Bonjour* already when the menu came) and ask politely for a more detailed description of the various dishes.

That alone will usually earn his wholehearted attention including his own recommendations for that day and a happy relationship throughout the meal.

Visitors to Paris, especially those who do not speak any French, often get into trouble by missing these important first steps. Treat a waiter poorly in France, you get poor service.

Of course, if you don't speak any French you are going to have to take your first steps mostly with hand motions. Most French waiters today speak a little English, especially if you try to speak French first!

What is really frustrating for him is a customer who refuses to communicate. If he can't communicate, he can't do his job properly. It is comforting to remember that only a fraction of the French intend to be rude. Most of the time it is that cool beginning of a discussion, an *engueulade*, aborted by the inability or unwillingness of the customers to communicate.

Some people I know communicate in all languages without any language skills. They have the gift of animation and imagination. If you lack such skills, learn some French! Then you can joust with everyone, converse and criticize. It's fun. The French aren't really so dour. They LOVE to talk. Encourage them.

The Fonctionnaire: Insecurity Breeds Contempt

There is a taciturn tendency among some French people, particularly among government workers (*fonctionnaires*) who deal with the public, especially in Paris. The negative attitude among bureaucrats stems partly from the fact that they have very secure, but low-paying, low-status jobs.

They don't have to be nice to anybody. Their job doesn't depend on it. On top of that, they get tired of people putting them down, treating them with low status.

In the section on French philosophy and politics we considered the sense of social classes that still exist in France. Class differentiation breeds deep feelings of resentment. People often try to "outclass" others, as they are unable to move upward in the rigid social system themselves.

It takes a very secure person to handle such "dominator" types gracefully but it takes just a little sensitivity on your part to avoid such posturing accidentally. Approaching a person as an important professional maintains your dignity and his. Your best tools when dealing with government employees are patience and respect.

Walk into a post office and tell yourself you have all the time in the world. Treat the person behind the counter as if he is doing you a favor. If he sees you impatiently waiting in line, you've had it. Blaming him for a long wait is no answer to anything. Treat him well and he will most likely treat you well.

In general, the ways to get through to people in public life in France are: (1) be patient, be sincere and try to establish a point of common intelligence, or (2) look innocent and lost and appeal to a person's sense of pity. If neither of these works, just realize there are curmudgeons in every culture.

The "No" Syndrome

Even more insecure than government workers are the lowly shop workers in large, impersonal places. These people are poorly paid, have very little status or job security, and even less job satisfaction. Their resentments can turn into a "put-down" game in a hurry. You are probably the 100th person asking the same dumb question that week.

My favorite is the "no" reflex. In Asia, people say "yes" first and mean, "yes, I heard your question" and then think about the answer. They are more anxious to avoid confrontation than to answer the question.

In France, people will sometimes say "no" even before you finish the question. What they usually mean is, "I don't know, that's not my job," or "I don't understand you," or "I'm busy now" or "I'm tired." The Frenchman doesn't exist who is afraid of confrontation. And the ideal of "service" doesn't exist in most large bureaucratic types of situations in France.

Here's how to get beyond those "no's". When you go into a shop looking for something in particular, don't ask the person sitting behind the cash register, looking bored. Her job is to take your money, not help you find things. Just say hello and move along. There will be someone on the floor more ready to help you.

If you don't know the word in French, look it up in your dictionary and try to say it, or show it to the store clerk. Or just describe it – that usually gets them interested. "Ah, a game!" they think.

I had one guy spend 15 minutes figuring out the kind of plant seeds I wanted when the only name I knew for them was "French Sorrell".

We discussed the leaf shape, size and color, the flavor, how it was eaten, if it had fruit ... He finally said, "AH! Oseille!" and brought me right to it.

If you still get that "no", find someone else, or if you are in a self-help place, just go look yourself. And the end of your search, the very last ditch approach, is to change the subject. Talk to them pleasantly about something else of interest in the shop, the discount price of something, the interesting utility of something, then slip in that question. If they really don't have it, they will probably at least tell you where to look! Often, though, you will get a positive answer this time, and they have exactly what you want. Why? Well, now you've made contact, had a conversation as equals.

But be warned. Since jobs are a reflection of class in France, everyone is class conscious. Don't go into a self-serve place such as Monoprix expecting a warm welcome and a personal tour through the aisles.

Real Rudeness

No matter how badly you are treated, if you have tried everything, being friendly, being interested, being grateful, being patient and the waiter or clerk still doesn't respond, your best way to deal with the situation is ignore it.

NEVER take it personally. It's not you, personally, causing this attitude. The French believe that underneath our class and cultural differences we are all humans. It is not you, this person finds distasteful, but life itself. Learn how to brush off a brush off.

Some people feel they must "put you down" first because they are afraid you will put them down. It's a kind of game in France. Insecurity in all of us runs deep; the French just show theirs more often. Americans, for example, are terribly afraid of not being popular.

No one has done an actual country survey measuring rudeness, but it only takes one or two brusque encounters with a French waiter to make a visitor feel intimidated by the whole country. This spoils things for everyone and makes it hard to stay cool and polite and impersonal. But you must.

Remember, these people don't hate you as an American/British/ Asian, in particular. They are equally or more rude to other French people. Here's how you play ...

The Rudeness Game in France

The waiter/clerk's position is, "I am feeling (choose any or all) tired/ insecure/pressured/bored, and here is this client I have to wait on. Yuk!"

You can play one of several positions:

1. You can take it personally, feel "put down" by this person and get resentful. Then, you lose the game before you start.

2. You can play, "You may feel tired/insecure/pressured/bored but I am here to get a little service, godamit. I can also put YOU down, I want this, this and this." With that, you must snap back with your order, in good French, and never make eye contact. Usually, the waiter/clerk will stonily fill the order, but he won't get any friendlier. That's a draw. (An unfortunate exchange in my opinion, which requires very good language skills, anyway.) The refusal to make eye contact can become a contest of this sort. I've seen a waiter and a client in a restaurant go through the entire ordering procedure, each diligently avoiding even looking in the other's direction. They managed to do it, so I guess that means they both "won", but what a hollow victory! After such an exchange, I'd check my bill carefully.

3. Your best position is the third one. You play, "I'm not going to be put down by you. I have time and patience and I am going to remain gracious and try to be friendly and ask for your advice and perhaps you will quit this silly game and realize that I am here for a valid reason and you are important to me." Nine times out of ten, you will win if you take this position, even if your French is poor.

Smile, But Avoid a Happy Face

Human beings are chameleons, at heart. If you remain gracious, not submissive, but open, sincere and reasonable, then you will often see that abusive attitude evaporate. You will get your own openness reflected back on you ... not in a wide, silly grin, but in an interesting exchange. Congratulations! You've really both won! OK, now you both have something to smile about, sincerely.

You won't always win the rudeness game in France. It helps to keep your feathers well-oiled so the occasional insult rolls off your back. As a foreigner, from the moment you open your mouth, you're vulnerable. Just because you can't return verbal abuse doesn't mean you are helpless. Be polite and see if they don't improve.

You will need to develop a critical eye, of course, and watch out for "tricks", especially things like short-changing and overcharging, but don't let this create paranoia. Real rudeness does not happen that often, even in Paris. When it does, there's no reason for you to be stumped.

RESTAURANTS AND THE FOOD MYSTIQUE

"Anyone with any sensitivity who doesn't want to live in Paris is out of his mind."

—American gourmet Craig Claiborne as quoted by Rudolph Chelminski in *The French at Table*

Why Things Close for Lunch

Following the sage advice of Richelieu in the 17th century, the most hyperactive Frenchman still spends a good chunk of his day sitting leisurely *à table*. The enjoyment of food and wine pervades all classes in France, and those two hour midday meals are still sacred, though international business standards are shortening the two hours to one and the four-course meal with wine to two courses with *eau minérale*.

Fortunately, there is not much else you can do in France from 12:30 to 2:30 pm. Most shops are closed (see Practical Information on "Hours") and everyone flocks to the restaurants. Join them!

In the old days and still so in the countryside, where wives are not working in offices and factories, the midday meal will be served at home. You are really lucky if you arrive in a small village at noontime, deep in the French countryside. Circle the main square, usually next to the church, and you will find at least one little restaurant serving glorious country cuisine and endless carafes of local wine for a pittance.

Warning! To indulge in a three- or four-course meal with wine at lunch time spells disaster for the remainder of a functioning day. Don't ask me how the French do it. Following a tiny breakfast of *café crème* and croissant, they eat luxuriously at lunch and/or dinner, yet still appear functional and always keep trim. I still need a nap after a typical French midday meal. I won't even start comparing figures.

But it's worth it. A lovely, almost holiday mood persists in French restaurants at noontime, with great conversation and special dishes. Eat up. Most restaurants close at 3 pm and will not open again before 8 pm. You won't have trouble filling the two hours, and you will be encouraged to stay as long as you like. No one is waiting for your table. Service is purposely leisurely, allowing you to enjoy each part of your meal, even reading the menu. Hurrying creates indigestion, as we all know, and is uncivilized in France. A professional restaurateur treats you as a discriminating guest and encourages you to linger, to feel "at home". Take a table outside and enjoy the scenery!

How To Order a Meal

Your best bet for quality plus price is usually the menu. A set meal at a set price, usually with two or three choices for every course, it is either written hastily onto a sheet of paper inside the regular menu, or posted on a chalkboard and displayed around the place.

French handwriting is slightly different from other countries and will take some getting used to. On top of that, restaurateurs often exercise their poetic skills in dreaming up names for their special dishes. Don't be embarrassed to ask. In fact, the waiter WANTS you to ask. It's his job to interpret, to recommend, to exhibit his command of the cuisine he serves.

We're talking religion here. Nothing is more important to a Frenchman than what he eats. A great discussion of the menu sets the tone for the whole event and establishes a good relationship with your waiter. (More on that in the next section.)

If you are vegetarian, feel free to ask for a vegetarian plate even if it doesn't appear on the menu. As with most things in France, everybody loves to do something special, something out of the ordinary, something that pushes the rules ...

If wine is included in the *prix fixe*, it will usually be a selection of the house wines, red, white or rosé. Otherwise see the *Carte des Vins* for more choices you'll have to pay extra for. (See the section on wines and their pleasures.)

For those without the iron French constitution, drinking water along with the meal helps moderate the effects of the wine and the food. Restaurants are required by law to supply a *carafe d'eau* if requested, but they will be much more responsive if you ask for (and pay for) bottled water. Either *avec gaz* or *sans gaz* (*plat*) or brand names such as Perrier (*avec*), Evian and Vittel (*plat*) ... the waiter will bring it in the bottle with a separate glass for each person.

Because everyone eats at the same time in France, the meal is a frantic event for your waiter. Watch that you are brought what you ordered and gently remind him if you do end up with something you didn't ask for. It's probably just a misdelivery.

Since restaurants in France are small, you can expect them to run out of things and have to substitute. Occasionally, especially in Paris, you'll get a bigger carafe of wine or a more expensive dish than you wanted, so the waiter can get a bigger *service* tip, which is calculated as part of the total. Usually, though, it will be an honest error or a necessary switch. Usually you will not be asked for your dessert choice until it is time. However, if there is a dessert that particularly appeals to you, you may ask the waiter to reserve one for you at the beginning of the meal, as they often run out.

After the meal, *digestifs* such as Cognac and *menthe* will be offered, as well as coffee or tea. A *tisane* is a herbal tea and comes in a wide variety of flavors that can really be great if your next destination is bed. All of these will cost extra.

At the end of the meal, you ask for an *addition* which will not be brought until it is clear you are ready to leave. To bring it sooner would

be impolite. Some less formal places leave the bill at your table, from the beginning, tucked under a plate or table cover. They will add to that, as you order, then sum it up when you ask them to.

Getting the bill is always a bit awkward. Try to catch the eye of your waiter as he races past a mouth or mimic a *"L'addition, s'il vous plaît"*. He'll usually get it.

Waiters don't respond favorably to finger snapping and hand clapping. (Would you?) Don't stand up and go to the waiter unless you are really in a hurry.

Check the bill for errors. Don't be embarrassed. The French do it, too. The number 1 is often written as an inverted V in French, a bit confusing at first. The 7 is usually crossed. The tip (*service*) will be included at 15% and leaving one to five francs more will indicate especially satisfactory service to your waiter. You don't have to leave anything extra.

Nearly everyone takes Visa or Mastercard now. Fill in the "total" box on your credit card slip when you sign it. Be sure to say *Au revoir* and *Merci* to your waiter when you leave.

Do's & Don'ts in a Restaurant

As a tourist, you will sometimes find yourself seated in a room full of other tourists. This is because foreigners tend to talk loudly at table together, forgetting that though people may not understand them, they can't avoid hearing them. This offends French customers. (It also offends me, especially if the loud ones are Americans, which is often the case.)

Please try to moderate your voice in public places! Especially when you are a restaurant, out of courtesy to others in a usually crowded space. Believe me, no one else is interested in your stories!

In spite of an active anti-smoking campaign, you will also find people smoking in restaurants, especially at the end of their meal. You can now ask for a "no smoking" section but as places are small, your best bet is to sit outside or by the door.

Things that are rude in France include bringing your own wine to the restaurant (their list isn't good enough?) and asking for a "doggy bag" (food is never as good as a leftover). Dogs, though, are usually welcome.

If you want to drink nice wines but can't consume a whole bottle in one sitting, come back another night and finish the bottle with another meal! If you are in a hotel with a restaurant for several days or you have found a favorite neighborhood spot, they will usually *garder* the half-consumed bottle for you. That is the degree to which they want you to feel at home!

CUISINE & CHARACTER BY REGION

> "*La destinée des nations dépend de la manière dont elles se nourissent.*" (The destiny of nations depends on how they eat.)
>
> —Brillat-Savarin in the 18th century

Nothing expresses the diversity of the French better than their regional wines and cuisines. I doubt any Frenchman would protest being "pigeon-holed" by his best local fare, so I have taken the liberty of "stereotyping" the regional personalities by describing some of their culinary specialties and relating those to local character.

This should be a fun way to help you learn some of the differences. (My apologies, of course, for the gross oversimplifications and overstretched parallels. Kindly remember that the French honor, above all, their individuality.)

Were it not for Good Food, who would Travel?

Whether you are doing business in France or just touring, learn something of the culinary details of the region you are visiting. Nothing holds the interest of the French better than the subject of food and wine, unless it is sex and politics, which can be touchy subjects in mixed company. Knowing a bit about the regional cuisine will add

to your appreciation of the meals and help you join in with the company you are keeping.

In the provinces, the family gets together regularly for major feasts: birthdays, weddings, baptisms, confirmations and holidays all demand a massive turnout and everyone will eat and drink his fill. There may be a hundred people at table and you may be invited along. The menu will include regional and seasonal specialties along with copious quantities of local wines. Often, at the end of the meal, especially among working-class families, the diners will tumble spontaneously into bawdy singalongs or poetry recitals. If you haven't been drinking, such excellent drama may lose something in the translation.

Cuisine 101

Learning more about the endless variety of French cuisines is a wise investment in the best that France has to offer. We cannot even scratch the surface here. For further reading I heartily recommend Anne Willan's classic *French Regional Cuisine*, my favorite source. (See "Bibliography".)

AOC

French law has strictly governed the quality of French food and wine since the time of Napoleon. The national system of *Appellation d'Origine Contrôlée* (AOC) recognizes wines, spirits, butter, cheese, poultry, fruit and vegetables which have certain qualities dependent on their origins and the way they are produced. When you see the "AOC" label on a food or wine in France, you can be confident that you are getting the real thing. The laws governing the production of these goods are more strict than anywhere else in Europe, or in the world.

The French at table. Though space is restricted, privacy between tables is respected with lowered voices.

In wines, for example, not only the specific acreage, but the number of vines per hectare (two acres) and the way the vines can be pruned is legislated and strictly enforced. The French place great value on their local cultural traditions, and their affection for them remains strong today, in spite of the invasion of McDonald's and Levi's. Thus, we can look at regional wines and cuisine as expressions of the personalities of their creators.

Normandy

Along the coast closest to England, the Norman countryside offers simple country fare quite similar to that of England, with an emphasis on pork and potatoes, creams and pastries. It's no wonder the Norman people are round and jolly. Indeed, they will remind one more of the English, with whom they have shared a common ancestry, since the Norman Conquests of 1066.

The rivers produce trout and the sea gives shellfish and saltwater fish, but like the famous soft cheeses of this region, Camembert, Pont-l'Evêque, Neufchatel and Livarot, much of the production is sold in Paris or abroad.

The spirit (*eau-de-vie*) of the region, Calvados, is distilled from the popular local apple cider. Benedictine also comes from this area, its flavor created from herbs found along the Norman coast, not from apples.

Apple pie is the favorite dessert. With a dollop of *crème fraîche*, the French cultured cream, it's enough to die for.

Brittany

Just below Normandy, the Breton region is most famous for its *crêpes*. The local grains did not lend themselves to breadmaking, and *crêpes* became the staple, used in everything from a main course to dessert. The Breton language, which is still spoken, is related to Cornish and Welsh, and like those people, the Bretons are an independent and self-sufficient lot.

101

FRANCE

NORTH-PAS-DE-CALAIS

HIGH-NORMANDY

PICARDY

Caen •

LOW-NORMANDY

PARIS •

ILE-DE-FRANCE

LORRAINE

• Strasbo

BRITTANY

CHAMPAGNE-ARDENNE

ALSACE

LOIRE VALLEY

CENTER

Saumur •

Châteauroux •

FRANCHE-COMTE

Dijon •

BURGUNDY

Poitiers •

La Rochelle •

POITOU-CHARENTES

LIMOUSIN

Cognac •

• Limoges

• Lyon

• Bordeaux

AUVERGNE

RHONE-ALPS

AQUITAINE

Agen •

MIDI-PYRENEES

Toulouse •

PROVENCE-ALPS-COTE-D'AZUR

• MONA

Nice

LANGUEDOC-ROUSSILLON

Toulon

The famous French cartoon strip, Asterix, is about the misadventures of some Bretons in the Roman era, when fighting the Romans (which they did quite successfully) and eating wild boar were the two main activities of life. This is not to say food is not delicious in Brittany, but the cuisine reflects the simple dignity of stone age menhirs which still litter the countryside. This is also the land of the artichoke and the cauliflower, rugged individuals of the vegetable family.

The fine white wine of Nantes, in the south of Brittany, the Muscadet, has a bone-dry simplicity that has endeared the world of wine lovers. Not fancy, but clean and honest. The *quatre-quarts* cake, made from equal portions of flour, butter, sugar and eggs, is similar to the American pound cake. Solid stuff, indeed.

The Loire Valley

The Loire Valley boasts what is considered to be the purest, unaccented French and is considered a cradle of French culture. Ironically, having so many of the royalty housed there over the centuries in their magnificent palaces has helped create the simple but very sophisticated cuisine. The fresh fish, vegetables and fruits of the rich Loire Valley are cooked to perfection, but their natural character never altered. Nothing heavy about the Loire wines and cuisine.

Food writer Anne Willan explains that King Charles VIII introduced Italian vegetables to his *château* at Amboise at the end of the 15th century. These included lettuce, artichokes and green peas, formerly unknown in France. The white asparagus, so popular in spring here, never see the sun. Among fruits are plums, apples, apricots, melons, peaches and pears. From these come fruit *pâtes* in winter and fresh tarts and custard cakes in summer. Plums were brought from Damascus during the first crusade and thrived.

The wines of the region vary from the crisp, clean and dry Muscadet of Nantes, the sophisticated, slightly sparkling Saumur, the tart red Touraines, and the petillant Vouvray. The character persevering here in both cuisine and character is a lightness and subtle sophistication quite unlike the heavier, creamy people of Brittany.

Cointreau, the famous liqueur of Anjou, gets its flavor from orange peel. The cheeses here are Saint Paulin and baby Gouda, mild and firm, as are the goat's milk cheeses like Valençay and Sainte Maure. *Charcuteries* abound, especially game *pâté* and *rillettes*, cooked meat mixed with *pâté*.

Ile de France (The Paris Area)

The area around Paris, for about 50 miles in any direction, holds 20% of the country's population and the vast majority of its foreign tourists. This is a pity, since they miss the wonderful splendor of regional cuisines. But they miss none of the raw produce.

"Paris has in abundance everything that could be desired," wrote Jerome Lippomano in 1577 (quoted by Rudolph Chelminski). "Merchandise flows in from every country. Provisions are brought in by the Seine from Picardy, from Auvergne, from Burgundy, from Champagne and from Normandy. Thus, although the population is innumerable, nothing is ever lacking. Everything seems to fall from the sky."

Now French cuisine and produce literally go up into the sky. The former market gardens around Paris have become suburban communities, so the food sources of all France now convene at the ultramodern wholesale market at Rungis, just south of Paris. From Rungis much of it goes to nearby Orly airport to satisfy the world's taste for French gourmet foods. From New York to Hong Kong, restaurateurs call in their next day's order of wild strawberries, mushrooms, endive, whatever is in season, and it is flown, that night, from Rungis.

Though Paris itself is not the culinary center of France, the Ile de France is known for its soft cheese, the Brie, as well as fancy pastries, potatoes and endive. The *baguettes* and croissants that make Paris so sweet smelling, are also a regional specialty, as are *béchamel*, *espagnole* and *hollandaise* sauces. But just as common, now, are

sauerkraut and *couscous*. Ironically, Paris is a collection of regional foods, but not of the regional cuisines, which must be adapt (with a compromise of integrity) to local tastes. To understand the regional variety, both of the foods and the wines, in truth, one must go around the country.

Champagne and the North

The world's most famous sparkling wine comes from chalk hills 100 miles northeast of Paris. There are wonderful sweet pastries that go along with the wine and come from the local sugar beet production. Verdun *dragées*, or sugar-coated sweetmeats, have been famous since the 13th century. The Flemish influence is also evident.

Also popular in the north are root vegetables: carrots, potatoes, onions elevated to masterful perfection in a *pot-au-feu*. The local cabbage is also elevated into elegant soups, braised for hot dishes and blanched for salad. Lamb, pork and beef are also important aspects of the cuisine.

Two cheeses, the *Coulette d'Avesnes* and the *Maroilles*, are famous, and the *andouillette* is a specialty. You'll find a more Northern European attitude here: more worldly, more attuned to cultural variety. Nothing expresses this better than the most famous product of this area, Champagne.

This remarkable improvement on what was a rather mediocre white wine produced on the cold chalk hills around Epernay has stunned the world. Almost 200 million bottles are produced each year, many of them selling for more than US$20 at retail. It's got to be good. The UK alone buys 10% of the production and the USA just slightly less.

The Alsace and Moselle

Northeast France, territory often disputed with Germany, is home of the *quiche lorraine*, an egg pie that seems synonymous with French cuisine. But the staple of the region is pickled cabbage (*sauerkraut*), hot potato salad and sausage, real testimony to the Germanic heritage, as is the Alsatian language, a German dialect also spoken on the other side of the Rhine. But there is plenty of French influence from the *pâté en croûte* and *mousselines*, and the Alsatians will tell you they are French, not German.

Pork is also a staple, from which a wider variety of sausages are made than in Germany. There is even a "sweet and sour" style of cooking meat with fruits here, dating back to the 16th century.

Goose is a favorite autumn dish, stuffed with apples or chestnuts. The goose liver is made into a *foie gras* that rivals Perigord's. In fact, this region is considered the source of forced-fed goose liver, credited to the Jewish community here, which needed a substitute for pork fat in their cooking and found it in goose fat. Fresh fish is often prepared cold, *en gelée*.

The wines of the Alsace are white, dictated by the cool summers. Both dry and sweet; they are low in alcohol and are considered by some to be the best whites of France. They are named for the grape rather than the location from which they come: Sylvaner, Riesling, Gewurtztraminer, Muscat, Pinot ... Beer, of course, is the other local drink, a lighter one than those of nearby Germany.

German-named pastries (*kugelhopf, kaffeekrautz, hirewecka*), *pain de Gènes* (almond cakes), *madeleines* and the *macarons de Boulay* are all famous local desserts. The clear *eau-de-vie* made with various fruits, Mirabelle from yellow plums, Kirsch from cherries and William pears, serve well as *digestifs* after these heavy meals. Sweet liqueurs, made from the same fruits, are recognizable for their characteristic fruit colors. These are considered medicinally beneficial.

The Münster cheese comes from a specific valley of the Vosges and gets its strength from the character of the local cow's milk. It goes well with Gewurtztraminer.

So this region has a Germanic character, lightened and complicated by the French influence. Expect some obstinacy in Strasbourg, but not much. After all, they are dedicated to their cuisine.

The Alps

Another region of France close to a border country, in this case Switzerland and Italy, also takes a part of its character from its neighbors. Hay and cattle are the crops here, Gruyère, Comté and Emmenthal cheeses being the results, and cheese fondue and cheese soufflé the evidence at table.

The staple meat, however, is pork, made into Chamonix ham and a variety of sausages. The fish from the streams are full of bones, so the meat is made into *quenelles*, or fish cakes. Many dishes are served in the gratin style, with milk and cheese. The walnuts of

Grenoble are AOC, and a liqueur is made, flavored with their flesh. Chartreuse is also from this region, a herbal liqueur flavored with saffron, cinnamon and mace.

Wines from the northern part, the Arbois, are great with Morels (*morilles*), and the other mushrooms of the mountain forests: *girolles*, *trompettes de la mort* and *cèpes*. The rich red Rhone wines, to the south, are marvelous with all this cuisine.

The Burgundy

South and west of Alsace, at Dijon, the Burgundy wine district begins. Here are the famous red Burgundian and Beaujolais wines, made from Pinot Noir and Gamay Beaujolais grapes, respectively, as well as the white Chablis (made from Sauvignon Blanc) and the white Burgundian chardonnays.

In this century, no other wines of France have had a greater impact in the world, eclipsing even those favorite clarets of Bordeaux. Dijon and Lyon have been gastronomic centers since the 14th century when Dijon became famous for its mustard.

Along with the wines are the tan Charolais beef cows, perfect for *bœuf bourguignon* and indigenous to this area, though now raised all over the world, and the famous chickens of Bresse. Wild fowl, frogs, snails and fresh water fish are also local specialties. The *escargots de Bourgogne* live in the vineyards, feasting on grape leaves all summer and hibernating under the vine roots in winter. They are usually harvested just a few weeks after they begin hibernating, when their systems are clean, but they are still plump.

From Nevers comes the *nougatine*, a lovely dessert. Lyon is a chocolate haven. The sweet *crème de cassis* made from black currants is the local liqueur from which the Kir, a dry Burgundian white wine with a tablespoon of the liqueur, is made. Among cheeses, there are the *Bleu de Bresse*, *Saint-Marcellin* and *Rigotte de Condrieu* all made from cow's milk. *Picodon* is a goat cheese from Montélimar.

The Auvergne

The center of France is less traveled than most, being the high mountains of the Massif Central. The cuisine is based on dairy products, pork, potatoes, cabbage and wild berries ... real country fare. Good, strong cheeses, uncooked and pressed up in the mountains, abound: *Cantal*, *Salers* and *Saint-Nectaire*. Two blues, *Fourme d'Ambert* and *Bleu d'Auvergne*, are also AOC.

The Limousin oak provides cooperage for Cognac and the Limousin breed of cattle, one of France's famous beef. Pork products and sausages are popular. "Given the climate," says Anne Willan, "the cooks of the Massif Central go for calories rather than finesse ..."

People of Auvergne are considered to be tightfisted. They come to Paris, work in dingy cafés and save all their money. Certainly they've made a killing with some of their products. The mineral waters of Perrier and Vichy spring from these mountains, around the old spa of Vichy. Badoit and Volvic are also locally produced and all are strictly controlled by their AOC. The Limagne valley is an original source for frogs, whose legs are still fried and eaten here, and known all over France.

Cognac and Bordeaux

Moving across to southwest France, the famous wine regions of Cognac and Bordeaux, is to visit a land uniquely mixed with British characteristics. In the 12th and 13th century, this Aquitaine region was part of England. Since then, when Bordeaux was the fourth largest city in England, it has been a cosmopolitan and prosperous center of trade.

Though the Bordeaux wines have been outshouted by the Burgundies, they are still unsurpassed. The great *Grand Cru* vineyards around the city produce some of the most famous wines in France, from the complex, dark reds of St. Emilion, Margaux and Château Mouton-Rothschild to the elegant sweet Sauternes. The crisp white Bordeaux from the Graves and Entre-deux-Mers are equally pleasing.

In cuisine, one returns to the oysters of the sea coast, which are raised at the water's edge, then brought inland to fatten and mature. They take their names from these maturing villages. The Marennes oysters have a green meat. The *entrecôte* of the Bordelaise complements the red wines, as does the St. Emilion chocolate charlotte.

The *Chabichou* goat cheese is remarkable and the Charente is both dairy country and home of Cognac, the great brandy of France, different from an *eau-de-vie* in that, after distillation from wine, it is aged in wood barrels, instead of crocks, thus adopting a golden color. *Foie gras* and truffles come from this area, as well as elsewhere in France, but the *truffe du Perigord* is considered the best. The Gascogne was home to Cyrano de Bergerac, the archetype of the Frenchman: chivalrous, generous, reckless, brave, irresistible to women, vain and boastful.

The Pyrénées

So far from Paris are the mountains separating southwest France from Spain, you would expect major cultural differences. The Basque people are still demanding independence in their mountainous homeland on the southwest extreme of the Pyrénées, high above Biarritz. They are the originators of the red beret, now synonymous with the French, in general, to outsiders, but still very much in evidence in the Basque country, along with a cuisine closer to the Spanish: red peppers, vegetables cooked with garlic and salted fish. Once the Basque people hunted whales in the Bay of Biscayne. Hot blooded people.

At the bottom of the mountains, in Béarn, is the hearty country fare of a *poule-au-pot*. (The famous béarnaise sauce was actually invented in Paris, though named for this region.) And *confit* is another: salted meat or game cooked and preserved in fat. On the other side of the Adour river is Armagnac, a grape brandy aged in wood barrels, like Cognac, but whose character is ever-so slightly sweeter. (In a blind tasting of 12 Cognacs and Armagnacs, I choose the latter, every time.) They even make pastries with it.

The local cheese, *fromage des Pyrénées*, is red-skinned when made from sheep's milk and black-skinned when made from cow's. Both are AOC.

The Languedoc

Originally there were two Frances, split by their languages and indicated by the way they said "yes". The *langue d'oil* to the north used *oui* and those in the south used *oc*. Today the Languedoc includes the Mediterranean coastline, west of the Rhone river, to the Pyrenees. They are most famous for their thick bean stew *cassoulet* and *bourride*, a fish soup rich with garlic and olive oil.

The land is so rich here and the sun so plentiful, they can get three crops of vegetables, but the most important crop is wine grapes. The Herault, Roussillon, Corbières and Minervois produce most of the basic red table wine the French love: immature and rough. Perhaps this is an unfair assessment of the people, themselves, however.

In the stark, poor hills above the Tarn, it's sheep country, as it has been for thousands of years. Anne Willan reports a *pot-au-feu* called *cabassol* made from lamb's head and feet. Economy is still a primary consideration in much of this area, in contrast to the Toulouse, now capital of high technology in France and home of the Concorde.

The candied violets of Toulouse are now a popular export item. And in the north, the Ardèche is home of the famous chestnut cream, *marrons glacés*, as well as home of the Roquefort cheese, made in limestone caves with sheep's milk and protected by law since 1411. (For the real thing, look for the little red sheep on the package.)

So what have we here? In the countryside, a simple, strong, direct farm folk and yet in Toulouse, all the sophistication of candied violets. The Languedoc is a fusion of the basics with the best.

The Provence

Home of the great seafood stew *bouillabaisse*, this is a cuisine of strong contrasts: peppery, garlicky main dishes made with olive oil, and balanced with fresh, cool tomatoes (only considered edible since the 19th century), fennel and eggplants. Ratatouille was born here. The herbs of Provence grow everywhere: lavender, rosemary, thyme, sage ... and anchovies, olives and capers add to the list of major flavorings. Melons and figs are AOC. There is abundant evidence of Italy here, both in the cuisine and the warm ways of the people.

The lovely rosé of Provence is also AOC, as are the deep reds and flinty whites, though it is the rosé that is my favorite, made from a blend of red grapes brought by the Romans and as old as Persia, which are quickly pressed and the skins removed to give that light salmon color. Light and full of humor, the rosé reminds me best of the Provençal lifestyle, as do Pernod and Ricard. Flavored with anise (licorice), the latter turn cloudy in water, like the outlawed *absinthe* and the Greek *ouzo* and the Arab *arak*.

The southern French people are considered lazy by Parisians, who give little credence to the laid-back ways of the Mediterranean coast. But with such lovely cuisine, who wouldn't spend all day at table? For more on Provence, see the films *Jean de Florette* and *Manon of the Spring*. Or read *Letters from my Windmill* by Alphonse Daudet.

If we haven't convinced you, by now, of the need to travel around France to get a picture of it, we give up!

Grand Cuisine

In their endless effort to organize and qualify everything, the French have developed complex systems to recognize good, better and best restaurants in France. The oldest and most famous, the Guide Michelin, was started by the tire company of the same name, to encourage motor touring back in the good old days (1933) when few people had automobiles. The Michelin guide comes out every year, giving one, two or three stars to the very best restaurants in France. Only a handful have three stars, and even one star puts the price out of most people's normal range. These restaurants must struggle hard to keep their stars, so you can count on quality, if not value-for-money. Great places to go on expense account.

The Gault-Millau guides also rate French hotels. Their system is newer and a little more complex, involving a series of one to four chef's hats (*toques*) separating traditional (*toques rouges*) from *nouvelle cuisine* (*toques blanches*). There are also the Bottin Gourmand and the Auto Journal guides. Plenty of recommendations to keep you well-fed and impoverished.

Wine and its Part in French Life

"A meal without wine is like a day without sunshine."

Most of the wine drunk in France does not fall into the AOC categories described in the previous section.

The stereotypical working-class Frenchman starts his day "killing the worm" with a shot of basic red wine plonk followed by an *express*, the thick, bitter concentrated coffee in the tiny cup. Every bar in France serves this peculiar combination, though it's mostly the older generation that adheres to the tradition.

Except for breakfast, however, no proper French person would consider a meal without wine. From the time a child is old enough to hold a glass, he is allowed to share in the enjoyment of this beverage at family celebrations, though he must be 14 to be served in a restaurant.

One million Frenchmen produce two billion gallons a year, one quarter of the world's total. They consume more wine, per capita, than any other people on earth. Alcohol kills more French people than automobile accidents. It is the number three killer after heart disease and cancer.

Although alcoholism is clearly a serious problem, overindulgence is not acceptable to most French people. You will very rarely see a

French person "drunk", either at home, at a party, or on the street unless he is in the category of "bum". A proper Frenchman may be a little flushed after a good midday meal, but he will not be staggering, or slurring his words, or ill.

How does this happen? The French have no secret of tolerance for alcohol. They consume a great deal of wine, but nearly always along with a meal. They take a glass or two each at lunch and dinner and skip the Anglo-Saxon habit of the cocktail hour.

Wine is not a typical cocktail in France and the cocktail party, in spite of its name, is not a Gallic institution. Before dinner at a French home or when you sit down in a French restaurant, you may be offered an *apéritif*, usually a wine-based sweet product like Dubonnet, or Vermouth (which is what the French mean when they say Martini). The current favorite is a Kir: a mix of white Burgundy wine sweetened with Cassis, a black currant liqueur.

Clear, sweet anise-based liqueurs like Pernod and Ricard, which become cloudy when mixed with water are Provençal favorites now offered everywhere. Otherwise, a little whisky over a piece of ice. Many today just prefer a *jus d'orange* or Perrier water before the meal. Ironically, for most French people, wine complements the food. The tannin in red wine melts the rich fats of French cuisine and blends deliciously with meats and vegetables.

Wine quality is not usually an issue of pressing importance to the French consumer. The AOC laws established by Napoleon guarantee a certain standard of quality and most people find that satisfactory. Don't be embarrassed to just order the house wine in a restaurant.

Of course, there are the "wine snobs" who analyze every nuance and can distinguish among the years and vineyards of the great Burgundies and Bordeaux, but you'll find many more of these among the English than the French.

In fact, wine sellers in France often complain of the lack of discrimination among their countrymen. The people who pay the most for French wine are the English and the other Northern Europeans. Consequently, most of the great wines of France are sold outside the country.

Simple red wine is cheaper than beer, by the glass, in France, both in bars and restaurants. It is everyman's beverage. Wine is such a basic part of life in France, people take it rather casually. Not like food.

A Frenchman will analyze and criticize his meal long before he'll worry over the similar subtleties of the wine served along with it. He will expect the wine to "fit" the meal, of course, but nothing more.

This is a shame, because French wines offer a wide range of characteristics. If you know a bit about them, you will enjoy being able to pick and choose from the wine list. And finding new wines is not only fun, it is a course in French geography. Most wines are named for the places they come from in France, not the grapes from which they are made.

Learning French Geography in a Glass

Wine making is a 2,000-year-old tradition here as varied and complex as the country itself. We'll get into some of the details of French wine, because it is such a remarkable product. But the best way to learn about the wines is to move around the country.

Most French people prefer the wines of their own region. Thus, many of the most interesting wines in France are consumed right in the villages where they are made. As you travel around the country, you will meet these wines and come to love them for their happy association with the people and the countryside from which they come.

If you cannot travel, or you return to Paris looking for more region wine adventures, you will find the "wine bars" of Paris your best bet. These are cafés and restaurants catering to the enthusiast of a particular wine region. The patron's intimate knowledge of that region allows him to gather the best vintages of specific villages otherwise unavailable, even in a good wine shop in Paris.

You can try them yourself by the glass or by the bottle. Order several different ones to compare the nuances of neighboring villages or different years. Simple plates of fresh country breads with *pâté* or cheese or *rillettes* will allow you the important experience of seeing how the various wines go with different foods.

How Wine Came to France

The Phoenicians first brought wine-making to France, following the Mediterranean coast, colonizing Marseilles by 620 BC, then moving inland along the Rhone River. Loving wine and planning to stay, they brought a variety of grape vines with them and planted them along their way. Some of them, like the Syrah and the Muscat, originated in Persia. All these grapes were vinifera, specifically for making wine. The Romans continued this civilizing tradition, 500 years later.

All the great wines of France are made from vinifera grapes: Cabernet Sauvignon, Chardonnay, Sauvignon Blanc, Merlot, Muscat, Pinot Noir, Johannisberg Riesling and Chenin Blanc. Often these are blended together, and until recently, the wines that resulted were known only by the name of the region in which the grapes were grown and the wine produced. Now, following an American custom, the French are naming some wines by their grape name.

Most of the wines of France are place-named, and those names carry real meaning. Since Napoleon's time, the regions in which the grapes are grown, the kinds of grapes used, and the grape-growing and wine-making practices, have been more and more strictly defined, by law. The tiny vineyards of Bordeaux which produce *Premier Grand Cru* wines sell for a fortune, although their drinkability may be well expired if they are more than a couple of decades old. This is the absurd end of the effort to sort out the good, better and best wines of France. But learning some wines by their place names, and finding ones you particularly like, are part of the fun of being in France.

Though wine collection and appreciation has developed a serious snob appeal, especially among the English, there is no reason to be intimidated about wine in France. Except for a tiny fraction of the huge production (those *Grands Vins* of France which are hard to find anyway), French wine is very accessible and strictly a question of your personal curiosity or preference.

Learning about the wines of France should be a light-hearted, haphazard trial-and-error experience, strictly for pleasure. There's not such thing as a "wrong" choice for a wine with a meal. The rule of thumb is white wines with white meats (turkey, chicken, fish, veal or pork) and red wines with red meats. But you don't have to follow it.

You might find a few wines you like better than others. You might find some sauces go better with a red wine even if the meat itself is white. It's fun to experiment. The French don't take usually their wines too seriously and neither should you. And if you do get a chance to enjoy the company of wine "expert" you will have to let him make the choices, anyway.

How to Choose a Wine

Say you are going out to dinner at a respectable, modestly-priced Paris restaurant. Your wine list, usually located at the end of the menu, will probably look something like this:

> *Vins Blancs* (White Wines)
> > *Sancerre*
> > *Muscadet*
> > *Pouilly-Fuissé*
> > *Chablis*
> > *Vin de la Maison*
>
> *Vins Rosés* (Rosé Wines)
> > *Tavel*
> > *Provence*
> > *Vin de la Maison*

Vins Rouges (Red Wines)
Bordeaux
Bourgogne
Beaujolais
Côtes du Rhone
Aude
Vin de la Maison

The *Vin de la Maison* in each category is the simplest, the house wine, and usually the least expensive of the selections. It is usually available by the quarter, half or full carafe – a full carafe being a litre container, more than one person can drink in a sitting.

Everything else on the list is the name of a place in France. Once you get to know the basic regional wines and learn the differences between a light red such as a Beaujolais and a heavy red such as a Côtes du Rhone, you'll have enough command to read a wine list in any but the most intimidating establishments. You can always ask the waiter for his suggestion. He'll be happy to provide it.

Most wines on the list will be sold by the bottle, though some, especially the reds, may also come by the carafe. A decent restaurant will open the bottle for you at the table, and let you look at the label to be sure it is the one you ordered.

If you order a carafe or a fraction of one, you'll have to take their word for it that they filled it with Bourgogne (Burgundy) and not Côtes du Rhone. A carafe wine will usually be near the bottom of its quality category, a little rough and unfinished, so the regional differences may be hard to tell.

The price of the wine usually goes up along with quality and popularity. You pay more as you become choosy about the particular wine you want to drink, especially if your favorite happens to be from the fashionable Bourgogne region. Don't go on price alone; in fact take some risks at the lower end of the prices offered, even the carafes.

There are many excellent French white wines beyond the best known, Chablis and Pouilly-Fuissé, but people know these names and order them and they are priced accordingly. In the more discriminating restaurants the list will get more complicated. Here the assurances of the AOC laws will help you by guaranteeing a certain level of quality from a Beaujolais village, whoever made it.

Most visitors (as well as the French) settle on a few regions they particularly like with particular dishes. For instance, I prefer a Bordeaux with a very good piece of meat but a Côtes du Rhone with just a steak in pepper sauce. With hearty country casserole or something in a tomato sauce, I'll opt for a Beaujolais or a Touraine red. With a fish course, I'll take a nice dry Muscadet over the fancier Burgundian whites any day.

Generally, more robust wines stand up to hearty fare. Lighter or more delicate wines are at their best with more delicately flavored dishes. Yet a complex wine can take either a very complex dish or a very simple one. There is NOTHING wrong with drinking a white or rosé with steak, if that's your preference! Don't be intimidated by those wine snobs, even if your waiter happens to be one.

Telling Wines Apart

So, let's start with the whites on our list. The differences between these wines are not great, but you may find you prefer one over another. Pouilly-Fuissé, named for a small village in Burgundy, will be the most expensive, because it has become popular as a recognizable French chardonnay among Americans. Chablis, named for a small region southeast of Paris that is also considered part of the Burgundy region, also specializes in whites made from chardonnay grape, but they are usually very dry, unlike an American chardonnay.

One option to these is the white wines from the Loire River valley. Sancerre will be a bit fruity and may be a little spritzy, made from Sauvignon Blanc. The Muscadet will be bone dry, made in this case from the grape of the same name, but very unlike a sweet fortified

American wine with the brand name Muscadet. There is a Pouilly in this region too, which is a lighter white, made from the Chasselas grape, not well known outside of France.

The house wine on our list will probably be a blend from the south of France, without an AOC and young, but drinkable with the meal, as was intended.

The rosé wines in France, especially those of the south (in Provence, for example) are actually the closest to those wines first made by the Romans. They are usually a blend of different red grapes, and the only reason for the light color is that the skins are removed when the berries are first crushed.

Most red grapes have white juice. To create a red wine, the wine maker leaves the skins in the tank after the grapes are crushed and as they ferment. It is the skins that give the red color and also much of the tannin.

So, in the Provençal rosé you'll find some of the character of a red wine, but it will be lighter and perfume-like. The rosé of Tavel, which is a village north of the Provence, in the Côtes du Rhone region, will have a more robust blend of red grapes. The house rosé will be a more simple wine, probably from the Provence but without all the requirements for an AOC.

Among the reds, you'll find a wider variety of flavors and prices. There is a constant debate between Bordeaux and Burgundy red wine lovers about which is best. They are made from different grapes. The Bordeaux wines, known as "Claret" in England, are almost 100% Cabernet Sauvignon grapes blended with 5% to 20% Merlot, a milder flavored red grape. The Burgundy wines are made from 100% Pinot Noir grapes. Both result, in good years and with proper aging, in intense, full-bodied wines. But both take time to mature. I always ask for the year when ordering one of these wines. Less than three years old, and they are too green to enjoy.

The best wines of each wine region of France have been further specified by their particular village of origin, some to their particular vineyards. The Margaux wines of the Medoc region of Bordeaux, for example, can only be made from the fruit of a few specific vines near that village west of the city of Bordeaux. Same for a Meursault or a Gevrey-Chambertin from those villages in Burgundy. As a result, each has developed a certain character that some serious students of wine can distinguish, blindfolded. But even they make mistakes. This is where we leave you to plunge into the complexity of French wines for yourself.

Back to our list! The Beaujolais wines are made just in the southern part of the Burgundy region, but from a very different grape: the Gamay Beaujolais. This produces a lighter wine than the Pinot

Noir. It can be drunk young. The *Beaujolais Nouveau* is the ultimate example of this, a wine drunk within a few weeks of harvest. But that is only sold in November and December and should be consumed cold and before the winter is over.

Properly-made Beaujolais wines are good for three years or more and are quite popular in France, with the best ones coming from the nine little villages and called Beaujolais-Villages.

Côtes du Rhone also produces very popular wines, more intense reds than Beaujolais. The most famous of these is the Châteauneuf du Pape. All the wines of this area are made from a blend of up to nine grape varieties. These are usually a good buy in reliably hearty reds.

The Aude region is a relatively new grape growing area and has not enjoyed the prestige of an AOC designation, which delimits its vineyard practices and its grapes. However, the good hot summers in the Aude produce abundant harvests with good sugar in the grapes, so the resultant wines have good character, especially for the price. They tend to be a little fruitier and more alcoholic than other French reds, and they are usually sold very young.

My pet-peeve about wines in restaurants, in France and all over the world, is that they are sold too young, long before they are fully developed. It is a waste of money to buy an expensive Bordeaux or Burgundy wine that is only two or three years old. There are plenty of good, inexpensive red wines to be drunk in France that are at least five years old.

To pay more for what is a "better" place name, but then drink the wine before it has a chance to mature is nearly sinful. Certainly, it is not good value for money. Often, restaurants do not put the vintage dates of their wines on the wine list. Some wines don't have a vintage date, but they are always the cheapest ones. Don't be bashful about asking for the vintage on any bottle of wine, other than the carafe wines, of course. Give a good white wine at least two years and a red at least three or four years to age properly before you drink it. You will appreciate the difference.

Chapter Six

CONSUMING THE FRENCH WAY

THE ART OF SHOPPING

There's nothing like shopping in France. The shops of Paris, like those of Tokyo, are designed to seduce you. The displays are so tempting, the arrangements so fresh and the products so unique, you will quickly begin to fall into the old lure of "price is no object". Exactly what they had in mind!

Shopping in the expensive parts of Paris (the 1st, 2nd, 7th, 8th and 16th *arrondissements*) gives a new meaning to the old term "value for money". The new 1 euro coin may be about the size of an American quarter, but it is worth as much as a dollar...only it doesn't buy as much.

There are few bargains in France. You really must shop carefully and compare prices. The French shopper has fine-tuned her skills to such a degree that if I see a crowd of people at a shop or stall, I get in the line. Even if I don't need chocolates or apples or new dinnerware that particular day, I know I'm going to get something rare in France: a bargain. Either that, or they simply sell the best chocolates/apples/dinnerware in Paris and they are having a sale and it is a great value, no matter what the price.

The French discriminate to the point of infinity. Don't be surprised to find a French person recommending only one *pâtisserie* in the neighborhood, when there are a dozen of them and they all look and smell equally wonderful to you. Many of my friends think nothing of going all the way across Paris for their favorite ice cream.

As you know from the Food & Wine chapter, Parisians are particularly picky about their food. They moan all the time about the declining quality, yet the rest of the world gasps at the wonderland of options.

Generally I consider food, wine and housewares a bargain in France. That old French concept of craftsmanship still exists and is reflected well in these products. But you do need to shop around for price. To get started, refer to such guides as Gault-Millau's Paris Shopping tome, which recommends shops for nearly every kind of product.

There are also a number of new books out for foreigners with a wide variety of sources for things you need if you are going to live in France. (See the bibliography.)

The only prices controlled in France are the basic bread (*baguette*) and pharmaceuticals. Everything else is free market and the

French take such liberties seriously. Some products are consistently more expensive in France: electronics (especially everything made in Japan, which are subject to a higher duty than other GATT country imports), cosmetics, furniture ... but then again there are delightful discount stores all around Paris, full of things you didn't need but can't resist buying "just for fun".

They'll get you, believe me. You WILL consume!

Queuing

The French understand perfectly well the concept of lining up and being served in order. However, there is in France a curious desire to resist following the rules. It's part of the way people express their "uniqueness". And the French concede that someone may always have a good reason to break the rules.

So when someone breaks the queue, or smokes where it is forbidden, or parks in a no-parking spot, well, he probably had a good reason. Let him go ahead. Anglo-Saxons will have some difficulty with this. Asians will not. But the first time you need to take advantage of this flexibility you will appreciate it!

Paying

In many shops and in the markets, you will often find a curious French system of paying that seems quite inefficient to many visitors, but is really a reflection, again, of the French ambivalence towards money.

You will inspect the products and make your order with one person, who then gives you a ticket or shouts to another person the price of your purchase. You then pay that other person, the cashier, the amount, sometimes not even collecting your goods until you return from the cashier. Even in the modern department stores, this indirect system prevails.

The reason for this is two-fold. It allows the person waiting on you to be more personable, to present the products to you without the unpleasant duties of exchanging money to come between you.

It also allows the boss to control the till. Usually the cashier is more senior than service personnel. Usually it is a woman and often she is the owner of the shop. Money exchange is a serious and delicate thing in France, so it should not distract your shopping experience. Instead it should be in the hands of someone with wisdom and authority.

You will find a strong sense of honor in shops in France. Products are often out on display in the streets whenever the weather is good, while the shopkeeper is inside attending to customers. One could easily lift and take whatever one wanted.

Yet the flip side of this honesty is a common short-changing practice. Count your change carefully and remember when you give a 20 euro bill instead of 10 euros that you get that extra 10 euros back! It's almost a game, giving incorrect change, and you are considered stupid if you let it happen to you.

Also watch for pickpockets on busy market days and in places where there are tourists. There is a common hoax around the Louvre, for example, whereby a guy in a car will try to sell you "his Italian leather coat". It might be one of a number of products, but it will always be the case where he is desperate for money to get back home, to buy gas, etc., etc., and he needs cash, any cash, you can give him for this product. Right, guy. Do I look THAT stupid?

Now, on to the variety of shops in France!

The Outdoor Markets

The open air markets of France are legendary and though a dying form of merchandising in the world, they are kept alive here by the vitality of both the products and the people who sell them. Most people opt for the predictability and convenience of indoor department store and supermarket complexes in the international we-have-everything-packaged-up-and-sealed-for-your-protection-and-convenience mold.

Here is how Rudolph Chelminski describes the French antidote to such uniformity, the open market:

"These market food-hawkers are a very special race, both the men and the women: hangovers from the Middle Ages who mix commerce, theatre and social commentary in an ongoing chatter that is designed as much to amuse and entertain as to sell. Like *chansonniers*, the best ones can draw crowds when they are performing well. For some curious reason which I have never been able to fathom, the stars of the trade, the ones most thoroughly infected with *joie de vivre* (and, I suspect, *joie de boire*) are invariably the vegetable and fish people. Butchers are vastly more reserved, as befits millionaires, as are the B.O.F. (*beurre-oeufs-fromage*) ladies, silently dignified in their white smocks, and the tripe dealers – the offal organ grinders, as they are known around my house – tend to lurk in the shadows at the back of their sinister shops, amid their treasured collections of ears and snouts and lungs and intestines and pancreases and other unmentionables which the French know how to make edible. When a vegetable man is in good form, his voice and imagination fueled by a few litres of antifreeze, the merits of his radishes, celeries or artichokes become positively epic, possessing every virtue known to humankind and instantly available at a miraculous price, which would be even lower if it were not for those criminals who run the government."

—from *The French at Table*

All over France and all around Paris the old "market day" tradition continues, thank goodness. Each neighborhood has a regular *marché* street at least once a week and each village will have a day when the merchants set up in the town square. Regular streets in Paris turn into block-long open-air bazaars. The most important market day is always Sunday morning, when every French family shops for the freshest goods for the most important meal of the week, Sunday afternoon.

Shopping here is quite different from going to the supermarket. You stand in line and wait your turn. Unless you see others doing it, you don't pick up the products. You ask for a kilo of oranges (everything is usually metric: kilos and grammes) and let the merchant pick them out. Some merchants now allow you to fill your plastic bag directly from the display.

No vendor offers shopping bags. Bring along a big canvas bag, or a string bag, to hold your various items. Once you become familiar with the way of doing things, you can start comparing the various produce quality and prices, and begin the serious business of bargain hunting along with all the other shoppers.

I tend to cheat and buy where I see the largest number of French women buying. Price haggling isn't done in these markets, until closing time or around 1:30 pm when the merchants stop for Sunday lunch. Then, in order to get rid of perishable produce, they will mark down certain remaining items. But everyone expects an exchange with you, even if it's just a comment about the fruit. This is really an opportunity for the flirtation of life that is France.

These merchants are professionals, in the true French sense. They love what they are selling and they love selling to people. Bring along your sense of humor as well as your appreciation of the French way. It's great fun to enjoy the variety and richness of these open markets, a living testimony to the French appreciation of all the sensual elements of food and of life. Most of them start around 9 am, so you can come for breakfast and linger on.

The Specialty Food Stores

The first one that draws the visitor irresistibly is the *pâtisserie*, where one finds warm croissants from 7 am and fresh *brioche*. At tea time, a wide range of French sweets lure the dinner guest.

Lord knows who consumes all of these in Paris. French men and women either have lightning swift metabolisms or buy these things to feed their dogs and cats. They are heavenly places no dieter would dream of entering. The *boulangerie* will specialize in the long *baguettes* of Paris, cooked twice daily and once on Sundays so no French person has to eat something as awful as day-old bread.

The fishmonger will clean your fish for you, after you have chosen it.

You needn't look far for a *pâtisserie* or *boulangerie* anywhere in France. You can smell them. If the weather is at all decent, the shopkeepers wisely leave their doors open, cooling the bakery room and sending tempting wafts of fresh bread out to potential customers. Pure seduction. At lunch time, there will often be all sorts of sandwiches, made up in advance, for the waist-watching French person or visitor. Better buy them before 1 pm, though, as these shops often close for lunch and some do not reopen in the afternoon.

Next to marvel upon must be the fish (*poissonnerie*) and meat (*charcuterie*) shops. Rudolph Chelminski has another wonderfully amusing passage in his book on the *charcuterie* in France:

"… the *charcuteries* rank along with the wheel, gunpowder and Catherine Deneuve as fundamental contributions to civilization. Literally, the word refers back to the cookers of meat – in medieval French, *chaircuitier* – but in modern terms it has come to mean a very special kind of artisanal food shop halfway between a butcher, where everything is raw, and the grocery store or supermarket, where everything is cooked, canned, conserved and industrially embalmed in one way or another. The *charcutiers* are more cooks than grocers, and what they sell is meant to be taken out and eaten at home or in the office. All of them offer the usual selection of cooked and smoked hams, of course, and sausages and cold cuts and pickles and even some canned and dried goods, but the heart of the *charcuterie* is in the dishes which the patron has cooked up fresh for the day: the whole chickens roasting on the *tournebroche* out on the sidewalk; the vats of the peculiarly bland French version of *sauerkraut*; the pork and veal roasts, and the *rosbif* French style, so rare that the middle is hardly cooked at all. Around these staples, artfully arranged in the front window and then behind display counters inside, are several cornucopias of salads, cold omelets, smoked salmon, scallops on the half shell with *béchamel* sauce, decorated with little crescents of *pâte feuilletée*: these and a score of other delicacies, all of them sultry and seductive and ready to go home with the first customer who addresses them a kind word and a small bank note. A *charcutier*'s front window display is enough to make grown men weep with pleasure and anticipation. I always carry a handkerchief myself, just in case."

You probably won't need a handkerchief, but do carry a shopping bag or large purse along for all the goodies they offer. Specialty shops in France do not offer plastic bags. You get those at the supermarkets.

Shopping for Cultural Specialties

No matter how good you are at coping with another culture, everybody wants to taste something from home, from time to time. Although most international cuisines have been adapted to French tastes, you can find the most authentic ethnic food shops in the areas where those people live.

- Middle Eastern food   19th and 20th *arrondissements*
- American food   the 7th and 6th and Champs Elysée
- British food   pubs can be found everywhere
- Chinese food   13th and 20th
- Greek food   in the 5th
- Indian food   Gare du Nord area
- Italian food   pizza is all over town
- Japanese   near the Opéra, on rue St. Honore
- "kosher" food   the Marais

Shopping for Things other than Food

The big French department stores, Printemps, Galeries Lafayette, Bon Marché and the rest, look very little different from Harrod's in London, Seibu in Tokyo or Saks Fifth Avenue in New York. They carry everything from toys to canned goods, but the main specialty is fashion and cosmetics.

In Paris, they cater to visitors, offering money changing services, export discounts, a travel agency and theatre ticket sales, and multilingual staff. A good place to go when you want to avoid culture shock and still shop!

FRENCH, ENGLISH AND US CLOTHING SIZES

Women's dresses, knitwear and blouses

F	36	38	40	42	44	46	48
GB	10	12	14	16	18	20	22
USA	8	10	12	14	16	18	20

Women's stockings

F	1	2	3	4	5
USA	8½	9	9½	10	10½

Women's shoes

F	35½	36	36½	37	37½	38	39
GB	3	3½	4	4½	5	5½	6
USA	4	4½	5	5½	6	6½	7½

Men's shoes

F	39	40	41	42	43	44	45
GB	5½	6½	7	8	8½	9½	10½
USA	6	7	7½	8½	9	10	11

Men's suits

F	36	38	40	42	44	46	48
GB	35	36	37	38	39	40	42
USA	35	36	37	38	39	40	42

Men's shirts

F	36	37	38	39	40	41	42
USA	14	14½	15	15½	16	16½	17

Men's sweaters

F	36	38	40	42	44	46
GB	46	48	51	54	56	59
USA	46	48	51	54	56	59

There are the ubiquitous big suburban discount stores in France, which have all the charm of these anonymous monoliths found elsewhere in the world. Even the French haven't managed to overcome their uniformity, though the products will be a bit better. And you can find bargains at these which will never be available in the little specialty stores. But even in Monoprix, Carrefour and the rest of them, you have to compare prices to get a bargain.

Chapter Seven

HOME LIFE

FAMILY AND THE LIFE CYCLE IN FRANCE
"In France a man's privacy is sacred – even on the street."
—Luigi Barzini, *The Europeans*

Like all cultures, the French have a unique way of seeing themselves within their family construction. Their view is quite different from the American view, for example, even though from the outside it appears to be the same.

Some of the differences have been brilliantly explained by Raymonde Carroll (op. cit.). In this chapter we try to introduce the

French family, as the French would see it, blending together some of Carroll's insights with those of others.

The Family

The French put family first. Family is a social cement and a specific, personal duty of each individual involved. Outside are public life, philosophy, politics, art and cuisine. Inside is family.

Although French people can be very romantic about "love", they take marriage and children in a very practical way. The extended family supplies emotional and economic support. Marriage is one building block of that extended family, not just something to fulfil one's personal dreams or emotional needs.

However, as Carroll notes, marriage is not the major threshold into adult life. Having children is. Children constitute the parents' obligation and link to the family and to the society at large.

Children are a joy to their parents, as they are in all cultures, but they also involve a serious burden of obligation to the respective families of those parents. (Asian readers will have an easier time understanding this than Americans.)

Children

Because children are a reflection of the parents' duty to the family, their proper behavior, especially in public, is very important. The old-fashioned ideas that children should be well-dressed and well-behaved, even that they could be "seen and not heard" are still upheld in France, though of course it is getting harder to do it.

Parents will reprimand their children in public, sometimes as much to show other adults that they are trying to do the job correctly as to really instruct the child. The French adore their children, but they show that affection with a firm hand and a seriousness of purpose.

After a certain age, love is not just a question of hugs and kisses. Young French children are carefully watched by the parents and their upbringing is of vital concern. The whole country gets behind the "back to school" chores in September. Parents are even known to go along to music lessons and sit in, monitoring the child's progress.

French parents are not playmates to their children, as in some other cultures. Their job is to civilize. The child seeks companionship among his siblings and other children. When there is a party at home, the children will usually be sent off among themselves, and they will be expected to work out their differences among themselves, the older children taking responsibility for the younger ones.

This way, they learn the function of roles like the "go-between" and how to work together, circumventing when they can the law as laid down by authority (the parents first, then later, the government, as we see in "System D").

At adolescence, the isolation of childhood is ended, the rules relaxed. Teenagers are rewarded with an apprenticeship into civilized society, with the freedom to experiment and explore. They are supported by the family and live at home, but each is allowed a remarkable degree of independence, compared to many cultures.

Parents and other adults will still correct and criticize these children, but they are generally allowed to go about their business. The "control" at this point becomes the family bond. The child's conduct always reflects back on the parents and the child is aware of this duty.

Children at this stage are encouraged to participate in discussions, to reason and to think. If he has learned his lessons well, he is now of a "reasoning" age and his own sense of responsibility is encouraged. High school students are even allowed to smoke in France, and will go out with their teachers to a café.

Parents will continue participate in the children's lives where they can, intervening on behalf of the children throughout the school years to university level and helping with that first break in the job world.

Because of this respect for their "independence" children who do not marry often continue to live happily at home. "The French support their children until they are stepping on their beards," says one British friend who has lived in France most of his life.

When children marry, the parents will often help them out with housing, furniture and other expenses. Once the children come of this new union, the cycle of care and belonging starts again, this time with the young parents starting their "civilizing" job with their own children.

Being a Child Yourself

In public, in the absence of the parents, other adults will quickly feel invested with parental responsibility. Remember, being adult is being a parent in France. This role, however, often plays itself out by giving instructions. Confused visitors about to make some error may find themselves being reprimanded in no uncertain terms by a total stranger. They may feel insulted, that they are being treated "like children". In France, this need not be taken as an insult.

By giving this personal, parental attention to a stranger, the French person is actually extending himself most generously, paying the stranger the compliment of parental concern. Criticism, especially in public, seems out of place to most visitors and, in any case, none of the French person's business.

I try to accept all criticism in France as given with the best intentions. There will be times that an insult is really intended, but generally, they are trying to help, and though they are not necessarily "friendly" in their approach, they are extending themselves to you to a degree that gives you a status higher than "stranger".

Going the other way with this approach, however, also takes some cultural sensitivity. Like most people, the French do not like to be blamed. There is a fine line between criticism for the future benefit of the actor and blame laid upon the actor for a result that cannot be changed.

Polly Platt, in her book, describes in detail the importance of not distributing blame in France. No matter who is at fault, the important

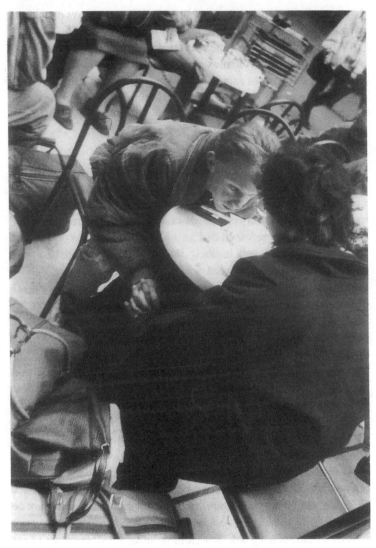

Young people are not considered adults until they have had a child.

issue to focus on is how to correct the problem or get around the blockade. This is a good Life Philosophy, generally, come to think of it.

Being a Couple

Since maturity means parenthood, young people, married or single, remain in an "adolescent" stage until a first child is born. This does not imply that sexual "coupling" is not taken seriously. The public pronouncement of a couple, inside or outside of marriage, implies a serious change in social category.

The relationship separates the couple, in one way, from their world of friends. After establishing themselves as a couple, the further intimate details of their lives together will not generally be subject for discussion, even among friends. Passion and intimacy between the couple is reserved for the two of them, either at home or for a totally anonymous situation (such as the classic Paris scene of a couple walking down the street locked in a kiss).

Being a couple does not mean they will do everything together and exclude their old friends, however. After the initial glow subsides, both in public and with friends, the couple will be expected to act in the normal, individual French way, expressing their opinions, showing their emotions and maintaining their circles of relationship.

In conversation, a partner may criticize the other without reflecting on the status of the marriage. To show the special nature of the solidarity between them, they may make each other the butt of their jokes.

Couples who argue issues when among their friends are considered to be acting normally, like individuals. The French say there is only one step between love and hate. Love is exhibited better by passion than by harmony. One displays indifference to one's enemies.

Harmony, which is an important public "image" for married couples in many cultures, can look like indifference to a French person. It might even indicate boredom in the marriage. And better ANYTHING, to the French, than being bored!

139

Aging

As parents age, they slowly (and not without protest) switch roles, becoming the responsibility of their children. While the relationships between parents and children are usually strong and important, the goal here is not to "be friends" but to be good in their roles as parents and children. (Friendships are a special category of relationships, as we will see in the next section.)

The parent/child role reversal can come quite early in life in France. When they reach 35, many young parents find their own parents already calling on them for advice and being obedient to their suggestions. As the French now prefer smaller families, they are also experiencing the nuclear family syndrome occurring all over the world. Older members of the family retire and move away from children and grandchildren. But the traditional Sunday lunch, with the whole family crowded together at table, is still a "command performance" wherever and whenever it is still possible.

Enjoying the parks is a family pastime in France, for locals and visitors alike. Dogs and children are welcome, but don't sit on the grass.

Evidence of this is still clear in the parks of Paris, which will be nearly empty on a Sunday morning, as families prepare the noonday meal. After lunch, they will flood with family groups ... all generations, strolling together, all dressed up and usually deeply involved in five or six conversations, bodies gesturing enthusiastically.

If a Sunday gathering is not possible, a long telephone call between parents and children is expected. See the section on the telephone for the way that 20th century invention has been adapted to the French sense of private vs. public.

BEING A GUEST IN A FRENCH HOME

You've been invited to a French home for dinner. BOY! Are you lucky! Few people, even French people, get such invitations. The French home is very private and very much family-oriented, as we have noted, so an invitation for dinner implies the offer of a high level of comfort with you and regard for you.

The size of Paris apartments, especially kitchens, limits the extent to which the French can comfortably entertain at home. Plus, expectations of the cuisine are so high, people usually prefer to go out.

This is something you can suggest to your French acquaintances. Never ask to visit someone's home if you haven't already been invited. If you need to stop by for some reason, telephone first.

If you are not invited to a French person's home, don't feel offended. Some of the most famous internationals who have lived in Paris, including Gertrude Stein and Henry James, had mostly other internationals for friends.

A century ago, Henry James complained that though he had been invited to the *salons* of Flaubert, and regularly met Zola, Maupassant and the other luminaries of the day (he also being well-known by then) they always treated him as if he were a total stranger, as if he weren't there.

He complained to his family, as he finally left Paris to live in London, "It is rather ignoble to stay simply for the restaurants," implying that he was never asked to French homes. But Henry James also said very positive things about his Paris life:

"You know, you get all ready to hate the French – it happens all the time when you live in Paris – then they'll turn around and say something or joke about themselves, and you like them all over again."

Being a Good Guest

Once you are invited to a French home, remember these basic rules, which the French also follow. They will help you get invited back and thus help you establish a friendship for life, for that is how the French are about their friends.

1. Arrive near the appointed time, but never earlier. Up to a half hour late is okay in the evening in a home, but not in a restaurant. You will probably be invited for 19:30 or 20:00, later in Paris.
2. Dress as you would for going out to a restaurant for dinner, the later the appointed hour, the more fancy the dress code. For the men, the code rarely goes beyond a suit and tie.
3. Don't arrive empty-handed. Bring a small offering, like flowers. Odd numbers are usually best, but avoid chrysanthemums (re-served for funerals), carnations (bad luck) or red roses (reserved for lovers and very close friends). You may also bring chocolates, another good choice, especially a small box of very good ones from a specialty shop, well wrapped. Most chocolate and flower shops will ask when you buy if your purchase is *"pour offrir"*, or "a gift". They will wrap accordingly. Unless you are in the wine business, it is usually better to avoid bringing wine. It might not suit the dinner and the wine, like the dinner, is usually the expression of the host's tastes and hospitality. To bring a bottle of your own may confuse the roles. The basic rule for gifts are: something on which the host would not indulge themselves. Something that appeals to the intellect or aesthetic. But nothing embarrassingly extravagant. A present for each of the children

sometimes works, and can be a good distraction. But usually at a home dinner the children will only appear to greet guests, then disappear for the rest of the evening. Adult evenings are the norm.

4. Allow time to finding the address. Remember that numbers on buildings in Paris increase very slowly. Number 20 may be a long walk from number 2, and often there is a 2bis following a building numbered 2 and before a building numbered 4, all independent addresses. Don't forget to ask for the door code, as most residential buildings in Paris now have front doors that are locked. There is usually a key pad on which you must punch the code before the buzzer will sound and the door unlock. The individual doorbells in the building will be inside, so you must either know the code or wait until someone comes by who does.

5. You will be welcomed into the living room and offered an *apéritif* ... or "cocktail" but it will probably be something small and sweet. Don't have the *faute de goût* (bad taste) to ask for wine. Wines will be served with the meal. Cocktails will usually be something sweet like vermouth (Martini in France) or a very short whisky. Let your hosts serve you and stand to receive your drink when it comes and to greet other guests.

6. There will be something to nibble, crackers or nuts rather than fancy American hors d'oeuvres (which on a restaurant menu usually means "assorted vegetables"). The meal may well be an hour or more away, but don't fill up. You'll be expected to eat a great deal later. Polly Platt, in her book *French or Foe?*, refers to this "introductory" period of the French evening at home as a very awkward one. It usually is. But once everyone arrives and the meal begins, everybody gets more comfortable. Life revolves around the meal table in France, not around the living room. While in the living room, you'll have to do your best to make everyone comfortable and relaxed. Tell a funny story about an experience you've had in Paris, especially if it makes you the fool.

7. One thing NOT done in France during this "warm-up" is a house

143

tour. The French consider it "showing off" to ask if you want to see their home. Although most of them by now know Americans expect it, for many it remains a breach of the private vs. public "face". It may also be that they haven't had time to clean up the rest of the house and would be embarrassed by its current state. So, awkward as this period is, stay where you have been placed. Don't even follow your host or hostess into the kitchen to help. You can offer to help, but take your host's decline literally. You are the guest and it is their pleasure to serve you. The only other room in the house you are likely to see on this visit is the toilet (the WC, not the bathroom, usually two different places). Likewise, don't help yourself at the bar (unless instructed to do so) and don't investigate more closely an interesting book on a shelf or object in a case. You are there to be an interesting human being, first. People are most important.

8. To be incorporated into the small friendship circle of this French acquaintance, you have an important duty. Your role tonight will involve participation in the conversation waltz, explained in more detail in the section on "Conversation".

9. At table, you will usually be "placed" by the hostess, so look for name cards or await her command.

10. Silverware is often placed downward. You should start with the pieces on the outside and work your way inward. The pieces above your plate are for dessert. Often, another set of utensils will be served with dessert and cheese. Each course will be served on new plates.

11. Wine will be served with the first course. Once everyone is served, the host may offer a toast to the guests or just a "*Salut!*". Once the meal has begun, if you know the host well, you may offer a toast back, otherwise just concentrate on the foods and wine and comment on them as appropriate. There will probably be several different wines, one for each course but the salad. Vinegar in the typical French dressing conflicts with wine.

12. Try eating with your knife in the right hand and your fork in the left. It's the French way and very efficient, especially with salad.

13. You may rest both arms on the table, between bites, but not usually elbows.

14. Break your bread off from the main loaf, don't cut it. Put the uneaten part or parts next to your plate, so they don't get soggy in the sauces, but leave your bones and bits on the plate, not on the table cloth or the floor. (I have a problem with this, as in Asia we move our discards off the plate, sometimes even off onto the floor.)

15. Sincere comments about the food and the wine are always a good topic of conversation. (But guard against false compliments – worse than none at all in France!) In a restaurant, you can be critical of the food; at home, of course, if you can't say anything nice, don't say anything at all.

16. Try to finish the food on your plate. It is a compliment to the hosts, as is a request for "seconds" unless the presentation of that course is obviously highly staged and difficult to repeat. The meals in Paris will be much lighter than those in the country. The very place your request for "seconds" will be appreciated most is in the country, where you are least likely to have room for it!

17. It is very tempting to soak up the delicious sauces in France with your bread. That is alright to do with company you know well, or if you see the host do it, but use your fork, not your fingers, to swirl the bread. The same applies in restaurants. But it is difficult to remember not to use your fingers, I know.

18. When you have finished a course, put your silverware together across the plate, fork up.

19. Courses will correspond to those in a restaurant. A starter (soup, a fish course, or a special salad), the main dish (*plat principal*), a green salad, cheeses, dessert or fruit. Wines will be served with all courses, except perhaps the salad, as vinegar fights wine.

20. As the cheese board goes around at the end of the meal, cut

yourself a share of the cheeses you want, maintaining the wedge shape. Take your share of the rind; don't take off the point. Watch how others cut if you aren't sure.

21. Peel and slice your fruit with your knife before eating it. (I eat the peel, usually, with apologies.)

22. An after dinner drink (*digestif*), either a sweet liqueur or a dry distilled product like Cognac, *eau-de-vie* or *marc*, will be offered. Now is the time to smoke, if you wish. Ask your host's permission, if no one else is smoking, and don't smoke between courses, unless others do.

23. Write a thank-you note or call the next day to confirm the pleasure of the event.

Accidents Will Happen

If you should have an accident in your host's home, say you spill something on a rug or break a glass, you will usually be immediately relieved of the responsibility of that damage.

No matter how valuable the object, your host will toss off the damage as nothing worth considering. This is good manners in France, where people are more important than things. (In the USA, a guest would consider it his duty to replace or repair any real damages he did.) In France, a host accepts responsibility for his guests as he would for his children. (Another reason, perhaps, why French people are slow to invite people to their homes!)

Offer to replace and repair your mistakes, of course, but don't be surprised if you are told that the Baccarat crystal goblet was "really worthless". If you do break something valuable, you might consider sending a nice gift, later, to express your appreciation for your friends' generosity.

Staying with a French Family

You've been invited to stay! How nice! Now you will see how truly warm and generous the French are. Now you will really be treated like family. Just a few thoughts, though, about when you first arrive.

In addition to those points mentioned above, remember to respect the household privacy. Don't wander into rooms with closed doors without knocking first. Leave the toilet and bathroom doors closed.

Don't help yourself in the kitchen unless instructed to do so. Ask before using the TV, stereo or radio. Do help out whenever possible with clearing the dishes and washing up.

The French are very concerned about disturbing their neighbors. As a guest, be particularly concerned about making noise including bathing late at night or speaking loudly in the hallways.

If you are a student going to live with a French family, do not assume automatically that you are being accepted as an equal. You are a family member, but still a "child" to them. Respect their rules and the private spaces in the home outside your own room. Don't let it all hang out unless behind the closed door of your own assigned space.

Because there is little private space in France, your presence will be a major impact on each member of the family. Try to minimize that impact, wherever possible. That is the basis of what the whole world knows as "good manners".

FRIENDS AND NEIGHBORS

Most French people establish friendships slowly, especially by American and Australian standards. As we have discussed earlier, this is not because they are unfriendly, but because a friend is a serious commitment, an extension of one's family responsibilities in life. So be patient and don't try to push your intimacy on people.

In Raymonde Carroll's book, she says a friend in France is what you would expect: someone who loves you like a sibling, whom you can trust, whose company you enjoy, who accepts you as you are. Friends help each other, but in France, friends are expected to do more than give support and sympathy. They are expected to help guide, correct and participate in each other's lives.

147

Anglo-Saxons can find French friends suffocating, always talking on the telephone, always discussing their personal problems in detail and always planning events together. Yet the French will rarely analyze the relationship between the two of you.

They prefer to let that "live" and discuss other things, like politics or art or fashion or events. Such discussions can lead to disagreements, but there is no threat here. Once a friendship is established, it will be strong enough to weather such storms. In fact, you will be valued for being honest with your friends more than for being supportive.

The French do not worry about being "equal" with their friends. They do not count favors or seek an equilibrium of the number of dinner parties or gifts one gives the other. They expect their friends to love them as family and the activity of reaching out to each other is more important than remembering who reached farther or first.

Carroll notes some interesting examples of this. A good friend calls another, saying she is exhausted. The friend immediately offers to come over, take the children, and allow her friend a few hours' relief. Pretty amazing, eh?

Friendship demands a great deal of commitment in France. Friends can call on each other, day or night, for the slightest reasons. The telephone becomes an extension of their relationship, another visit, another chance to connect and conversations are rarely short.

French people will call each other, right after they get home from a party together, if they think of something they forgot to say, or they have a bit more news. Between friends, a telephone is a line of love. When a friend calls you on the telephone, he will rarely introduce himself, expecting you to recognize his voice (and thereby confirm yourself: if it wasn't really you, you wouldn't know who he was.)

French friends often do things together several times a week. They will introduce their circle of friends to each other and attempt to combine the two circles as much as possible.

As you do become friends with a French person, you can expect to be pulled into his close circle, meeting his other friends, and included in their activities. You will then be expected to fulfil some of these emotional obligations and commitments yourself, as the French expect of their true friends.

That's why the expansion of the friendship circle is slow in France. Each of us has limited amounts of time and energy, so we must limit the number of people with whom we can be true friends. Counting many people as "friends", and therefore being very "popular", is not the French ideal. It is quality rather than quantity, here.

Compliments

French people are very conscious of their surroundings. You don't get cities like Paris or countryside like the Loire without making a conscious effort. So the French take seriously the impressions of other people. They don't like false compliments.

Commenting on a pretty dress, a new pair of shoes, or new haircut is a natural thing to do. But different cultures respond to this commentary differently.

Anglo-Saxons are taught to say "Thank you" when they receive a compliment, implying, "Thank you for making note of me, how kind you are." Compliments are more politeness than commentary, here.

In the East, a compliment is usually denied, meaning, "Oh no, I really am not that good and you are too kind and good to see how lowly I am." Compliments aren't usually given, just because they are awkward to receive.

But since French people compliment not to be polite, but because they really have an opinion, the reaction they expect is different from either of the above. Your response should reflect your appreciation of that person's opinion.

Just to say, "Thank you," is to imply, "Thank you, yes, I agree my dress is terrific." Too pretentious.

Instead, a proper reply is something like, "Oh, do you really think so? (with no sarcasm intended) I'm so glad you like it!", implying you admire and respect their opinion, and so accept this lowly dress as better, by that measure.

Making Your Home Among the French

While we are on the subject of home life, it is important to mention some of the expectations the French will have of you, when you are living among them, other than on the intimate level of "friend". Here are some tips on how to be a good neighbor, as well as how to keep up with Les Duponts.

Your first relationship in a building will probably be with the *gardienne* who is usually a woman paid to live on the ground floor and care for the needs of the tenants. She will usually have her family living with her, though her husband may work elsewhere, and she tends to things such as the mail, deliveries of goods, the maintenance of the ground floor facilities such as garbage bins, gardens and brass polishing.

Having a good relationship with the *gardienne* (or *concierge*) makes life infinitely easier in France. You can usually establish a good relationship by a friendly manner and thoughtful remuneration for any special attention you get, as well as Christmas and Easter bonuses, which usually should be anywhere from 50 to 500 euros, depending on your rent and the number of ways you are using her services.

The *concierge* will also often be a good source for other service people you need: plumbers, electricians, carpenters. She usually knows who is around and who has done good work in the past in the building. She will also have good neighborhood shopping tips.

The people she cannot help you with, very much, are the neighbors. These relationships are far more delicate, partly because of the special attitude the French have towards friendships described above.

Because you are living at very close quarters to the other people in the building and they cannot become friends with most of their neighbors, you must maintain a certain respectful distance from them.

They will show you how. This distance involves a polite acknowledgement of their presence, when you meet in the hallway, stairwell or elevator, but a respectful silence beyond that. The coolness allows both of you your privacy. It is not a "put down" or rude. It is polite.

Certain considerations will be expected of you. You will want to hold the door for anyone coming in behind you (as most people do, even in the *métro* stations in France).

You will avoid making any unnecessary noise in the public areas of the building, as well as in your own quarters, if that noise reaches other apartments. (Floors carry the noise of footfall and chairs scraping, for example.) Though you are in your own private space, you will be expected to behave in a way that assures everyone else their comfort and privacy, as well.

Sooner or later, you will begin to make better friends among your neighbors. Like all friendships in France, these will take time. Even in the countryside, you will find people hesitant to step forward, at first. Speak French and be patient. Remember the French love to be amused and you are probably a fairly capable person at doing so.

Meanwhile, you will probably experience bouts of loneliness, especially in the middle of Paris. Here are a few suggestions for combating this problem:

1. Go to the movies. All movie houses discount their prices on Mondays. Read *Pariscope* or *L'Officiel* for the details.
2. Ask your friends to come visit (few will need to be asked twice) and look up friends-of-friends, who are often glad to meet another international with whom they share some friend in common.
3. Join English-speaking organizations, as suggested in the appendix of this book, to get involved in activities that will teach you more about the art and history of your area.
4. Get yourself established as a "regular" in one of your neighborhood restaurants. They will make you feel welcome when you are eating alone. They will even set you up with other interesting "singles" so you can have an interesting conversation as you eat.

No friend is a better and more loyal one than a French person, but like all good things, they need time.

Chapter Eight

BUSINESS IN FRANCE

MONEY AND BANKING

"L'argent n'a pas d'odeur." (Money has no scent.)

The French have a very uncomfortable relationship with money. They relish expressions of sensuality in nearly all its forms, yet they find the subject of money indecent … the opposite of the stereotypical Anglo-Saxon. Socially, of course, "old money" is more respectable than "new money" and third generation nouveaux riches are distinguished from those coarser first generation nouveaux. Still, the topic of money is usually not discussed casually.

Although French people dislike talking about money, yet the LOTO, a lottery game, is popular among men and women of all ages over 18. Tickets are sold wherever the sign is displayed.

It is not polite to ask someone what they do to make money. No French person wants to be judged on that basis. This is quite difficult for Americans and Asians to understand. In business, no particular status is awarded to a person based on how much money he has or how quickly he has proven he can make it.

In Hong Kong and New York, money is the measure of all things. In France, it is more likely to be held against you. Much better to come to France as an author or professor or musician and be amusing and enlightening, if you seek social acceptance. We do not suggest avoiding making money in France. If you are here to do business, you will find the French ready and willing. But it will help to recognize this ambivalence towards money from the moment you start buying things in shops and negotiate with the banks and especially when you begin dealing with the world of office relations.

First rule to remember: DON'T ask people what they DO!

The Euro

France, together with eleven other Western European countries, introduced a new unit of currency on January 1, 2002: the euro. The currency is available in eight coins (2 euro, 1 euro, 50 cent, 20 cent, 10 cent, 5 cent, 2 cent, and 1 cent) and seven bills (500 euro, 200 euro, 100 euro, 50 euro, 20 euro, 10 euro, and 5 euro).

Despite the overall success of the transition to the euro, many French continue to speak of prices in terms of the former currency, the franc, especially in large sums. Thus, it is useful to know that 1 euro is worth approximately 6.56 French francs (fixed rate).

Opening a Bank Account

Banking is made as discrete as possible in France, to avoid everyone's embarrassment over dealing with it. French banks look more like second class airline offices and French banking personnel dress down, some even wearing blue jeans, and seated comfortably, almost out of view.

Most banks use an open counter design, creating as casual a situation as possible between you and the person handling your money. The major security effort is at the entrance, where you will often have to go through two doors, each opening only when the other is closed. If a bank robber comes in, they simply trap him as he leaves, between the doors.

To open a French bank account, you must be 18 years old, have a valid piece of identity (passport or *carte de séjour*) and a proof of residence (telephone bill or *Electricité et Gaz de France* bill). Most banks offer both savings accounts and checking accounts.

Foreigners are allowed to hold money in a French account, as long as you can show it came from outside the country, or that you have a *carte de travail* that allows you to earn money in France.

You will receive your checks in a few days and your *carte bleue* (CB, the name used in France for any credit or debit card) in a couple of weeks. Most banks link your CB card to the bank account in a debit system, so when you pay with your CB, the amount is deducted automatically from your checking account the next month.

You can also use the CB card as a cash card at money machines all over France, if you ask for a PIN, or personal identity code number. Some bank accounts, especially at the post office, limit the number of withdrawals you can make in a week, and some machines charge for withdrawals. Some savings accounts, like the *Postépargne*, offer both check writing and cash cards.

Many people in France have their salaries deposited directly into their bank accounts and their monthly bills, like EGF, telephone, etc., are deducted automatically. Automatic deductions are postponed until you have had ample warning, by mail, that they are going to do it. They are an easy way to get your monthly money chores done.

It is a major *faux pas* and a serious crime to overdraw a checking account in France. Thus, French checks are readily accepted everywhere, often without a piece of identification, making a French account a very convenient thing to have. As the *carte bleue* and other credit and debit cards become more popular, though, these are preferred. However, take care in punching in your PIN number in public view.

Cash for Travellers

Bank transfers between countries are ridiculously slow and expensive and travellers checks cost both when you buy them and when you sell. These days it is best to use international credit and debit cards like Visa and Mastercard when you travel.

They work in most cash machines around the world, using the same PIN number you use at home. Most credit card companies won't charge you for this service and most banks honor the best rate of the day on the exchange. Just don't lose it!

OFFICE AND BUSINESS RELATIONSHIPS
Learning to Work with the French

"As internationalists, we have, indeed, tremendous power, and our home-country business skills alone are no longer sufficient in themselves."
—Robert T. Moran, "Cross-Cultural Contact" column in *International Management Magazine*, July 1985

Now that we've said a little about the French approach to money, we plunge into a far more complex subject of inter-cultural relations in business: how you work with the French.

Philip R. Harris and Robert T. Moran's book *Managing Cultural Differences* is the bible of cross-cultural understanding for Americans doing business abroad. Moran, an American who has lived and worked in France, encourages cultural diversity in business, both to get a better global approach towards the marketplace and to enlarge the pool of management resources. But he admits there are disadvantages working outside one's own culture, including a more complex decision-making process and the risk of poor communications. Much is being written on this subject. EuroDisney has been an excellent microcosm of cross-cultural miscommunications. See the section at the back of this book on "Culture Shock" and also the suggested reading list on this subject.

Hari Bedi is an Indian expatriate working in Hong Kong. He suggests five C's in doing business internationally: continuity (a sense of history and tradition), commitment (to the growth of the organization), connections (where social skills and social standing count), compassion (balancing scientific and political issues) and cultural sensitivity (a respect for other ways of doing things).

These are the skills you'll be working towards, in doing business in France. Forget capitalism as your first priority; it is cultural sensitivity you need most now. The French don't really respect capitalism, just as they don't automatically respect a person based on

157

his professional accomplishments. Individuality and personality count for much more among the French.

Connections with your company's French branch will put you several steps ahead, when you come to France to do business. The local office can help you with the logistics of work visas, office supplies, as well as local communication and transportation skills. But even with a French office as your helping hand, don't expect to feel "at home" in the beginning.

Many things, visible and invisible, are different in a French bureau: from the paper clips to the filing containers to the standard size of the paper to the way meetings are conducted.

If you are used to the American 8.5 x 11 inch standard of paper, you will find the rest of the world uses an A4 standard, which is taller and narrower by nearly an inch. Likewise, the storage of files is handled in boxes rather than file cabinets, and American paper doesn't fit into them.

When a meeting is called, it will be very formally conducted, though the appointed hour may be more flexible than you are used to. Obviously you will have to start doing business, now, in the French language. You may notice that those pleasant French associates who spoke English so well during your brief visits to France in the past now take you along for lunch and speak French the whole time. Many of the office staff will turn out to be not as comfortable with English as you had thought originally.

From the instant you arrive, your language skills will be challenged. You should start now, gearing up on comprehension skills, both in language and in the silent rules of the French way of doing business.

Remember the description earlier about the star patterns in French life. Expect things to be different and you won't be so easily discouraged. No matter how good your language skills, you can expect to find it difficult to communicate. You must deal with a new game of personal relationships. You must learn what motivates a French person. For whom does he feel he is really working? Your affiliations and achievement orientation may be vastly different from his.

Less emphasis is put on individual performance, on the spirit of competition, and on one's identity as a worker in French offices, more on cooperation and flexibility. Doing several things at once and even holding several conflicting opinions at once is not unusual for a French person, nor is it considered inefficient or illogical. Remember those circles!

Robert Moran compares working internationally to fighting with two swords. At the same time as we use the personality traits that have made us successful at home: aggressiveness and competitiveness, for example, we have to learn to use a second sword of gentleness, cooperation, indirectness and commitment to relationships.

The French are not so oriented towards competition; they are innocent of the Puritan work ethic. Yet they are very conscious of job security, social status and being judged as an individual. Time is less linear and the value of time is not measured by money alone.

Thus the very traits that had been your strengths may become weaknesses in France. Harris and Moran describe the rigid structure of French organizations. Authority is more centralized, most individuals in the company have less authority and so decisions are usually reached more slowly. To defend one's position in the system, one may build walls of protection, rather than take aggressive action.

Listening and observing will be your essential skills. Several projects may be going on at once, with the same staff, and only the central authority will be capable of communicating ideas to everyone. You will need to carefully analyze the pattern behind the activities. Your relationship with each member of the team may be a more important concern than controlling organizational decisions. You gain trust and respect through your ability to work with others.

Many international firms are realizing that profound cultural differences separate their organizations in different countries, even though they may share a common language of business. There are hundreds of different scenarios that will illustrate these differences in France, but it helps to know a few in advance.

Firstly, don't depend on the telephone as a means of serious communication with people you don't know well.

The Telephone As Enemy

Your business relationships in France will probably start on the telephone. This is unfortunate, for though it is the same basic instrument and functions the same way as in other parts of the world, the telephone in French culture is not considered trustworthy. The lines work fine. People are just not comfortable speaking across them to strangers, even in French. Raymonde Carroll devotes a whole chapter to this subject in her book *Cultural Misunderstandings*.

When you first call an office or shop, you will often get the impression that you had better hurry up with your questions, that you are taking valuable time away from the person on the other end. They will ask for your name before they volunteer any other information or service, and they may only give their first name back to you, thereby remaining safely anonymous.

The French like to put off the moment they must commit themselves as long as possible. The telephone pressures the person answering into making a commitment he may not be prepared to make. Meanwhile, it distracts them from their real work at hand, their desk papers and the people around them.

A telephone call is similar to having someone knock on your door, unannounced, but worse. At the door, you can use the peephole and see who it is. You can say you were just going out. You can also get an idea of that person by watching his facial expressions; you can figure him out a bit. On the telephone, none of this is possible. French people feel very vulnerable and many respond poorly to telephone calls from strangers.

Unless, of course, a French person wants to complain. In that case, he will be more quick to use the telephone than go in person, as the threatening aspect of the telephone is to his advantage. So many people use the telephone only when they want to complain. Another reason a bureaucrat may not want to pick up the phone when it rings.

So, use the telephone to make appointments and when you must, but try to keep most of your business activities on a direct, face-to-face basis, or in writing, the very favorite way for the French to conduct business.

(For using the telephone with friends, that is a whole other story in the "Home Life" chapter of this book.)

Company Acquaintances

The French do not usually seek friendships among their business relations. They prefer to pick their friends on the merits of their personality, not their relative usefulness in business. Within a French company, structured patterns of authority prevent casual friendship, anyway.

When working in the French company, it is better to be pleasantly surprised by a co-worker's generosity and warmth than to expect it and be disappointed. Don't take it personally. That Gallic coolness is a necessity of French life, which places far more burdens on friendships once they are established.

This sounds contradictory. On the one hand, office relationships are very important, but on the other hand friendships are rare in offices. The distinction is between the levels of commitment.

Few office workers will offer the ego-building emotional support you might have enjoyed at the home office. Regardless of your success and track-record, you will be considered with suspicion, at first, in France. You may represent the higher, central authority of the company, on whom all is blamed and to whom little is credited.

Your secretaries may not be comfortable having lunch with you, since French firms tend to be strongly hierarchical. Office relations are important but delicate in France. There is a constant tension between the functions of the job and distinctions among the job descriptions. Although the French firmly believe in the ideal of equality, the social structure remains quite rigid, by American standards, for example.

Always use the *vous* form among business acquaintances and never use first names, even with your own secretaries, unless the French person suggests it. If you are unsure whether a woman is married or not, use *Madame* rather than *Mademoiselle*, as the latter also implies a spinster (an unfortunate state among the family-oriented French).

Avoid any but the most polite and patient approach to fellow workers, and be sure your business letters follow the formal French code. That handshaking exercise we described in the section on "Nonverbal Communication" symbolizes both the importance and the formality of relations in a French office. The handshake implies a degree of equality among the French, but not a great degree. It is made with minimal intensity or pressure, with little eye contact and it doesn't necessarily imply comraderie. Everybody does it, because some gesture of equality is important. But it isn't sealing a friendship.

Office Behavior to Expect

Security is the essential concern of the French office worker, more than job advancement or office comraderie. Though he will take his five weeks of paid vacation, he will rarely take a day off without pay. He will stick to his desk, his job and his position.

If you are coming from the home office, you will be treated with a certain esteem. You will be expected to respond accordingly. Trying to establish a back-slapping, hail-fellow-well-met comraderie around the office is not going to work. Remember the star pattern. Your job is to uphold your part of the web of office relationships, according to the French expectations.

Take each of your relationships at the office as unique and delicate, being careful not to accidentally strain the links of communication and function before you can recognize them.

Don't try to impress people with your accomplishments or abilities. Boasting is condemned in France. Try to direct attention away from yourself and towards an understanding of the specifics of your role in the business at hand.

Watch for subtle signs of class distinction in your co-workers. Respect these roles by maintaining yours. Your first goal is to learn to work with these people. Don't let someone's haughtiness put you off. The French play a class distinction game with each other all the time (see the section on "Getting Respect"). Once people feel secure in their role with you, they will not feel the need for posturing. As with the waiter, your job is to help make them feel comfortable by establishing that role. Then you can work together effectively.

As you begin to understand office politics better, you will come across a system of connections call the *piston*, which is the way French describe being pushed forward in one's career by a helpful superior. This is quite popular in France, a way of seeking out the "cream" in a group. It is not always a successful approach. You will find fresh starters beginning at different levels in the company, depending upon their *piston*. As in most of the world, connections count.

On the other hand, you will find people clearly above you who are deeply respected just by virtue of where they went to university. Polly Platt has a wonderful description of the French education system in her book *French or Foe?* that explains why those French *diplômes* mean so much.

Business Meetings & Negotiating

Business meetings in France are formal. There is a strong sense of protocol. Proper demeanor is critical. The person who takes charge of the meeting is the central authority. His job is to hear all opinions and to reach some compromise that is deemed fitting to the overall plan.

Though decisions are made from the top, during the course of the meeting, all opinions should be aired. Each person must be careful not to overstate his case, lest he take time away from someone else's opportunity to speak. (Refer back to the section on "Conversation".)

But everyone should get the chance to voice their opinion and discussions may get far more heated than they would in your business meetings at home. The person chairing the meeting will usually remain passive, listening.

The French consider negotiation as they would a grand debate, according to Bob Moran. At the conclusion of such debate, the French reason, well-reasoned solutions are to be found. Yet often after such a heated debate, nothing spectacular will seem to have been concluded. Sometimes, in what seems to be mid-debate, the subject may change completely, leaving one whole issue hanging.

Don't worry. Such airing of opinions is an important part of solving a problem. A great matter will take a great deal of time to consider. It is impolite to insist on one's opinions being agreed to. Agreement is not necessarily the goal of the discussion. By airing opinions, an appropriate and favorable compromise will result … eventually.

Let's break for lunch.

Having Lunch

> *"Ventre affamé n'a pas d'oreille."* (A hungry stomach has no ears.)

Lunch is a great place to establish good relations with the French. Few would consider a meal without wine and this gives everyone a chance to relax and get to know each other, putting the office problems aside. In fact, the general rule is, no discussion of business until the cheese course!

Often the subject of work will not even be discussed. Lunch is a time for enjoying the senses and the intellect, for feeling alive. There is more to life than making money. Lunch is a good example. Arriving at an office for a meeting just before lunch hour will not endear you to a hungry worker, nor will you find him very responsive immediately after a big lunch with wine. If you are trying to establish a good relationship with this person, suggest lunch, instead.

Taking each other out for lunch is a common gesture among business acquaintances in France and most French people will not protest your treating, if you state your desire clearly in the beginning. In better restaurants, the waiter will look around the table and decide which person is supposed to pay the bill.

That person will get a dollop of wine in his glass before the waiter leaves the bottle on the table. If you are paying, make sure you accept that dollop of wine from the waiter!

Drinking wine is one of life's pleasures in France, but inebriation is unacceptable. A bit of wine relaxes everyone and helps get the conversation going. If you don't want to drink and you are not paying, you don't have to accept the first glass, but it is more gracious to do so and sip it slowly. Order a bottle of water, as well.

At table with business associates, don't be surprised if the topic turns immediately to politics and your views are requested. Politics raise passions and inspire the intellect ... just the ticket for lunch time entertainment, to the French way of thinking. Now they will find out of what stuff you are made!

Your opinions need not agree with anyone else's, but you better be ready to defend them! Criticism of institutions and ideas makes better conversation material than agreement. The goal is stimulating discussion, a meaningful outlet for the intellect.

See the "Conversation" section of this book for topics to avoid. Generally you want to discuss things that allow everyone to participate.

The French often take two hour lunches, to talk as much as to eat. The negative side of these great, long lunches is the hours following. It takes two hours for a glass of wine to work its way through your system. So unless you will be able to take a nap after lunch, don't drink more than a glass or two during the meal.

The French are habituated to this noontime diversion, but even they are drinking less these days and taking more Anglo-Saxon-length lunches. It is unfortunate, as there is nothing so rich in cultural pleasures as a lengthy French midday meal.

FRENCH LAW IN YOUR LIFE

"Men are born and remain free and equal in rights."
—Jean Jacques Rousseau

French law dates from before the Revolution, to the 17th century reign of Louis XIV whose adviser Jean Baptiste Colbert centralized all power in the palace at Versailles. The Grand Plan of French democracy was described by Rousseau, above, but the Napoleonic Code, the basis of French law today, followed the example of Louis XIV and set a centralized approach into stone.

The Napoleonic Code has made for an enormous mountain of bureaucracy in France, and accustomed the French to filling in endless forms and giving the government information on every detail of their lives.

This will come as a bit of a shock for people from less administratively inclined countries.

Whether you are getting a driver's license or trying to find a job, you will be dealing with the unique and complex legal organization of France. The bureaucracy tries the patience of Job. But don't give up, there is method in the madness.

The French also complain about the hours of waiting in line and difficulty of getting answers from French bureaucrats. Just take three deep breaths, expect many detours and bring some good reading material along to read while you are waiting.

Also be on the lookout for *le système D*. The French take pride in their ability to *débrouiller* bureaucracy, that is to "untangle" it by resourceful means. There are many ways to do this. Parking in Paris is a good example of this, as we will see in the section on taxis and driving. But the best way is to have a friend.

For starters, you will need to come to France prepared for bureaucracy. Starting at home, be sure to bring with you: your driver's license, your marriage certificate, your birth certificate, any advanced educational or professional degree certificates you've earned, your international student ID card, lots of copies of your passport photo, copies of all your bank accounts and credit card numbers, and copies of receipts of all your major purchases which you are bringing with you, including home computers, stereo systems and other electronics. (See the "Home Appliances" section to avoid bringing products that won't work in France.)

There is a great book you should buy before you move to France. Called *At Home in Paris*, it is written by the Junior Service League of Paris and partly sponsored by Disney Europe, whose employees no doubt found it very useful. It covers hundreds of details of getting on in France that we have no room for here. (See Bibliography.)

Government Rights

While you are living in a democracy in France, there are some people more "equal" than others here. For one thing, the police have the right to arrest and detain you as they deem proper. Always remember that in dealing with them. Never argue with a policeman unless you want a night in jail.

As in many countries the tax authorities can deem you guilty until proven innocent when it comes to paying taxes. I have several horror stories that confirm this. In my own case, I was sent a written notice while abroad in Hong Kong that my small *chambre de bonne* in Paris would be emptied of its furniture in order to pay back taxes I "owed" in a small village in France I have never even visited.

Friends in France rallied for me and called the office involved, finally discovering that another woman with two of my names was the offending party. I had to write a letter and send a copy of my passport to prove I was not the same "Sally Taylor" they were looking for!

In another case, an American friend in Paris accepted the mail of a colleague who had recently left the country. *Lettres Recommandées* began arriving for the friend from the tax office in the town where he had lived. The friend said to ignore them. Then one day my friend returned to his flat to find a notice on the door that HIS furniture would be removed to cover back taxes if they weren't paid up in 48 hours.

Again, he called the tax office involved and tried to explain that the man they wanted had left the country. No luck. Again, he had to prove he was not the man they wanted!

Women's Rights

You will note that the quote at the beginning of this section refers to the rights of "men", not of "people". The original Napoleonic Code gave few rights to women. It is only since 1923 that women have had the right to open their own mail and only since World War II that women have had the right to vote.

However, French law protects women in many ways. The Government provides maternity and child care as well as abortion on demand. After a protest by anti-abortion groups in France, the manufacturer of the world's first legal "abortion pill" took their product off the market. The French Government made them put it back on, arguing that it was an important medical advance for French women.

A woman alone with children holds all rights and obligations for the family, unless it is decided differently by the courts. Women who have a third child are rewarded with extra home-help allowances. But marriage and courtship are more formal and both marriage and divorce procedures more complex. A woman keeps her maiden name all her life, legally. She votes and pays taxes under that name, but rarely does she use it socially.

The role of women in the workplace is still more conservative. Though small, entrepreneurial family businesses are a tradition in France, the male head of the family is still the norm and that authority carries through into the business world. There are growing numbers of exceptions to this rule and in principle the French believe in equal rights for women.

In reality, though, both women and men celebrate the differences between them. This enthusiasm for the opposite sex helps balance out the power structure better than any equal rights laws could. The French make an important distinction between "sexy" and "sexist".

Sending a Registered Letter

Something in writing carries more weight than a personal visit. A registered letter is binding legal proof and people feel bound to respond to it. In general, when doing business with any agency or company, it is always best to send a letter (in good French). Next most effective is to send a fax. To sort out some complicated things, of course, you must go in person. Knowing someone, or making friends with someone in the office you are dealing with will make a big difference, so avoid getting mad and getting "even".

Legal Logistics

Catherine Kessedjian, a French lawyer specializing in the legal needs of English-speaking internationals in Paris, graciously provided the material for the rest of this chapter. Additional material is available in books dedicated to some of these matters in the Bibliography.

Visas and Work Permits

If you plan to stay in France for any period over three months, you must organize things in advance. Your goal will depend on what you want to do while in France. The best way to go about this is to visit France as a tourist and consult with a lawyer there to assess the feasibility and administrative procedure for your return. Find a lawyer experienced in both business and immigration law, as the laws relating to foreign residency rights change quickly and often. (See the book *Working in France* by Carol Pineau and Maureen Kelly.)

All internationals who do not belong to the European Union or other special countries and who want to reside in France for more than three months must first obtain a *visa de long séjour*. That will require two visits to the French Embassy or Consulate responsible for your home country.

The first visit is to pick up the forms, the list of documents to be filed and the list of medical doctors accredited by the French Consulate. Then, when all documents are filled in and the medical examination complete, you must go back to the Consulate to file the formal request, with all your justifications in hand.

Here, the waiting period begins, up to three months, usually, during which time you must remain in your home country. Once the visa is granted, you may enter French territory and immediately present yourself to the local *Préfecture* to file for a residency permit. The same documents filed to obtain your visa will be needed. Once you've got the visa, as a student, for example, you cannot ask for a residency permit as a *visiteur*.

There are two kinds of residency permits: the *carte de séjour temporaire*, the maximum validity of which is one year; and the *carte de résidence*, which is a ten-year permit with full working rights. In a few cases, you can be granted the *carte de résidence* immediately, but usually you will first be granted the *carte de séjour temporaire* under one of the following statuses. For all of these, you will need proof of a clean police record and a medical examination.

171

Etudiant

To be accepted as a student you must show pre-registration at a university or graduate school, at least 600 euros in monthly revenue from whatever source, a prospective place of residence in France, and medical insurance, if you are not eligible for student social security.

Visiteur

(not to be confused with "tourist") You must show a minimum revenue of 1,200 euros, a private medical insurance (preferably French), a place of residence in France, an agreement not to work in France either as a salaried employee or in any profession for which special authorization is required.

Employee

If you are a salaried employee, your prospective employer must file a contract, written on special forms, and various documents, depending on each case, with the Labor Administration. To be sure this is done properly, a specialized lawyer is highly recommended. One copy of the contract, stamped with the authorization, will be forwarded to you. The employer will have to pay a special one-time tax based on the salary paid the employee.

Trader

Whether working as a sole proprietorship or as the manager of a corporation, if you do not hold a *carte de résidence*, you must be authorized by the authorities.

To do so, you must provide the bylaws of the prospective corporation, a detailed explanation of the business project you plan, proof of financial feasibility and good experience in the field, and proof that you have never been bankrupt before.

Family member	If you are married to an international already authorized to reside in France, you still must apply, in France, for your own residence authorization. This is done through the *Office des Migrations Internationales* (OMI). If you are married to a French citizen, you will be granted a *carte de résidence* with full working rights after one year of marriage. Before then, you have the right to reside and even work in France, if you find an employer.

In general, after three years of residence, if your status has not changed, you may be granted the *carte de résidence*. This does not apply to students.

Renting Laws and Tenants' Rights

Apart from commercial rental contracts, which are handled differently, the basic regulations for housing contracts apply, whether or not you are a French citizen. In some cases, you may sign a one-year lease, but the standard length is either three or six years. The tenant must give three months' notice of quitting. The owner, six months.

Commonly, the owner will ask for some guarantees (proof of revenues, a guarantee from a relative, etc.). A two-month rental deposit is normal, but more is illegal. Fees and expenses of a real estate agency must be split equally between tenant and owner.

It is very important that a thorough, written appraisal of the apartment or house be done before you sign the lease and before your departure, so that the owner cannot claim damages and keep the deposit. This is called a "contradictory" at which both parties or their representatives are present.

You must ask for closing bills from the EDF and the telephone company and pay them, before leaving, otherwise the owner has the right to hold the deposit until you can prove you have paid all the bills.

You must insure your own belongings as well as the apartment or house against fire, water damage, etc. You are also liable for taxes related to the apartment. A tax of 2.5% of the rent must be paid monthly and a flat *taxe d'habitation* must be paid by the tenant who inhabits the apartment as of January 1 each year. That amount depends on the size and location of the building.

Buying Property

Very few restrictions remain for non-French people buying real estate in France, except in certain areas or certain types of property (farm land and protected cultural property are the common examples). Deeds must be prepared by special lawyers called *notaires*, though any lawyer can advise you on real estate law.

Taxes for the registration of the deed and, generally, expenses related to the purchase of the property, are paid by the buyer. Apart from the fees paid to the real estate agent (which are calculated from the sales price), you must expect to pay an extra 10% of the property price if the property is to be used as a habitation and 20% if the property is to be used professionally. This is the estimate of the registration taxes and expenses previously mentioned.

However, there are some considerations to be made when putting such property into your will. An excellent book by Vivienne Menkes-Ivry, *Buying A Home in France*, describes all the details. In another called *Living in France* by the Association of American Wives of Europeans, the legal aspects of wills are detailed.

See the Bibliography for these and other helpful resources.

ESTABLISHING A BUSINESS IN FRANCE

Your embassy in France, or the French Chamber of Commerce and Industry (CCIP) will be able to help you in establishing a business in France. The CCIP publishes a booklet in English describing the basics of French law regarding businesses here. Ask for *How to start a business in France*. It gives you, in a very Anglo-Saxon manner, a step-by-step approach to administrative formalities, but you should certainly consider private legal assistance, as well.

Company Structures in France:

Entreprise individuelle	This is the equivalent of a sole proprietorship in US law, and the owner's personal and business assets are both liable. A spouse may become a partner by registering, as well.
S.A.R.L.	A minimum of 7,500 euros and two to 50 shareholders are required for this kind of company. Shareholders' liability is limited to individual contributions.
E.U.R.L.	Similar to the S.A.R.L., this allows the manager to limit his liability to his individual contribution while maintaining financial control.
S.N.C.	General partnerships require no minimum capital and the partners have the status of traders, but each is jointly and separately liable for debts.
S.A.	This is either a privately-owned or a fully public company, with a minimum of 37,000 euros capital, at least seven shareholders and no maximum. If it is fully public, the rules are more strict.

Subsidiaries, Branches and Agencies

If you want to establish a subsidiary company of one currently existing elsewhere, you also have some further choices. The subsidiaries are autonomous legal entities, economically dependent on the parent company. Their managers must obtain a *carte de commerçant étranger* or a *carte de résidence*, depending on their nationality. In some cases, they must also file a declaration of investment with the Treasury Department before registering.

Your company can also set up an agency or branch in France, for whose debts the company is totally liable. For this, you must register with the Trade Register, provide two certified copies of the company's Memorandum and Articles of Association translated into French, provide the name of the manager of the French branch as well as the birth certificate and French registration of all personnel.

A liaison office is even more informal and registration is not required, as long as you are only establishing contacts, handling publicity and collecting information in France.

Commercial Licences and Employee Requirements

If you are not French and planning to operate as a sole trader, a partner of an S.N.C., a manager of an S.N.C., S.A.R.L. or French branch, subsidiary or liaison office, or the general manager or chairman of the board of an S.A., then you need either a resident's card, an EU passport or a commercial licence.

If you are not holding an EU passport, your ability to work in France is strictly controlled. If you are being assigned by your company to work in France, or you are coming to France to work for a French concern, you must get a visa before you arrive from the nearest French consulate or embassy.

For individuals seeking to live or work in France, it is essential to get good legal advice before you arrive. For more detailed reading, see the Bibliography and Recommended Reading at the end of this book.

Chapter Nine

PRACTICAL INFORMATION

GIVING AND GETTING DIRECTIONS AND INFORMATION
On the Street

"A map without a compass is a useless thing."
—Charles Stockton

One of the first things that will happen to you in France is that you will need directions. Most travelers carry a map and if you don't speak French you are best to carry one, too. If you do speak French, you will find French people endlessly willing to give directions.

When a Frenchman gets lost (and many do, especially in Paris) he will be likely to ask you for directions, himself. This will be done with hesitancy and apologies for disturbing you (*Excusez-moi, Monsieur, de vous déranger, mais ...*). A French person will stop a total stranger on the street and ask for advice on where to go, though he wouldn't dream of making small talk with a person waiting in line with him at the grocery store. So this will probably be the first time a French stranger volunteers direct contact with you. It's a bit flustering and exciting, but stay calm and handle this carefully.

If you speak French, you now have a chance to participate in your first verbal waltz. Your interlocutor will wait patiently for your answer. If you don't know exactly where he is trying to go, send him off in the right direction and suggest he ask someone at the next intersection. If you are completely in the dark, the best thing is to turn and stop someone else walking by and ask him or her to help you both. When a French person stops to ask you directions, you should feel flattered: he or she is putting himself at your mercy, making himself vulnerable to you, by asking for your help. He is exhibiting his real faith in you, as a human being.

You now hold his trust in your hands. It is your responsibility to either provide the information he needs or find someone else who does. Etiquette demands you not leave this stranger until he is on his way, feeling better informed. If you just say you don't know and walk away, you've kicked the poor guy when he's down.

In turn, if you ask directions of a French person, you must give them the courtesy of listening to their whole answer, however long it takes. Give your thanks and head off in the direction they've advised, even if you know their answer was wrong. If you don't at least start out in the direction advised and continue until your adviser is out of sight, he may well race after you to correct your "error". French people have been known to give the wrong directions, rather than shirk the duty of a reply. They are not trying to trick you, but to fulfill the obligation. So pick your person carefully.

Here is how one French friend describes how she picks someone to ask directions from: "I ask a man or woman who looks intelligent. Not anyone old and slow, who probably doesn't leave the area very often and won't be able to organize his thoughts quickly. I look for efficient-looking people, serious people carrying an attache case, for example, and walking confidently. I don't ask young people; they might be too shy or too fresh." When you find your target, begin with the famous phrase, *Excusez-moi, Monsieur, de vous déranger ...* Then ask your question.

The Map Shock

Or course, if you don't speak French, you are going to have to rely on a map and a compass. It is often overcast in France and the compass will help you establish "north". If you are lucky, someone will stop as you look at your map and offer to help you, using English. Looking at a map in France is a clear signal someone is in trouble.

The French don't like to look at maps, generally. I love maps, and instinctively when I am asked directions in Paris, I used to reach for my map, only to find the French person waiting for my reply now has a look of something between despair and horror on his face. He may even be desperately looking around for another stranger to pull into our discussion. He didn't want a map, he wanted an answer.

The French tend to prefer asking a person for information. They don't like referring to maps, guidebooks, train tables, even directions for an appliance they've just bought.

There is good reason for this, according to Raymonde Carroll: a map gives a great deal of information that is superfluous to the problem at hand. A person, on the other hand, is likely to give only the information need to solve the specific problem. Efficient!

For the same reason, the information area (*renseignements*) at a train station will be quite large and usually jammed with people who have taken a number and are waiting patiently for their turn at a window, even though the answer to their question is probably displayed on a time table among the *horaires* display-racks nearby.

Such faith in human beings and unwillingness to cope with large amounts of extraneous information has created a breed of official French information-givers that can frustrate map lovers like myself. I often feel that people in France are not giving me all the information I need. This is probably my fault, more than theirs. They are trying to be efficient and give the minimum. I, of course, want to know all the options. Typical Anglo-Saxon!

Getting Information from Official Sources

The way you ask people for information is very important in France, especially if those people are considered the experts. As an international speaking poor French, you create a problem that puts your information-provider immediately on the defensive.

He may not understand your question and therefore be unable to give you an answer. He loses "face", as they would say in Asia. You have asked him for help and yet you have not been able to explain adequately what you need. Frustrated, he may become impatient or surly, adding to your troubles. Even though he is there to help you, a French bureaucrat is sensitive to frustration, especially when it comes to job performance. Here are some ways you can avoid a total breakdown in communications.

First, organize your question. Even write it down: where you want to go, what time, what class, and when you want to return. Include in your question a request for fare reduction, if possible. Remember that NO additional information will be volunteered.

Approach the railway/bank/postal worker as a person doing you a favor: *Excusez-moi, Monsieur, de vous déranger ...*

Admit your predicament: you need help. This person, though he is getting paid to do it, is actually putting his own self-esteem on the line for you. Don't think, "It's his job." He's a human being. You have a problem. Not him.

Also, don't ignore all the printed information available. Some of us like maps and the French give great detailed ones. Ask for the *tarif* at the PO and the *horaires* at the train station. Many answers are there. Most French people prefer to go in person to an office to obtain information or clear up a problem rather than calling on the telephone. The telephone, as we will learn, creates an intimacy that is intimidating to the French when they are dealing with strangers. It puts them off and makes them unwilling to provide more than a minimum of service.

At the office (*bureau*), you wait in line, giving the person in authority his due, then you have a chance to establish yourself in a proper, human way. By calling in, you are butting in line, bothering the person who must answer the phone, and generally starting off on a very bad foot, especially if your French isn't fluent.

There are exceptions to this, for example, airlines. They are used to doing everything by telephone. But airlines are a cultural exception everywhere.

Once you've established a rapport with the person waiting on you, and you've explained clearly exactly the information you want, you will get a reply that is probably less than what you would have liked.

Never mind. Thank them very much and move away for the next person. If you have another question, line up again. If you have enough for the time being, congratulations! Do not insist on dragging out the painful process with more questions and a reflection of the options while holding up the line. Make your decision, let the guy act on it, and go elsewhere to reflect. No one else is interested.

Life is a constant series of decisions. Everyone is sympathetic to that. But the rest of the world is not your personal psychologist.

HOURS
The Lunch Hours
It is a nine-to-five world, but much of France still takes *le déjeuner*, the midday meal, quite seriously. Many shops close during the middle

181

of the day for an hour or two. However, restaurants, the post office, the banks and the *supermarché* are sure to be open between 12 noon and 3 pm in Paris. In the countryside, only restaurants will be open.

This in no way implies that the French don't work hard. Shops take a break for lunch and often won't open in the afternoon until 3 pm, but they will stay open until 7 pm or 8 pm.

Offices usually reopen after lunch by 2 pm or 2:30 pm and stay open until 6 pm or later. You can find people still at the office until 8 or 9 in the evening. Many Parisians eat dinner late, at around 10 pm and even accept telephone calls until midnight!

But, hey, it's the lunch hour! Relax and enjoy a nice, long midday meal along with everyone else. (See the chapter on Food & Wine.)

Take note of the opening and closing hours and plan to do your shopping errands in the morning or later in the afternoon.

Shopping Hours

Taking into consideration the lunch hours (anytime from 12 noon to 3 pm), shops in the major cities open from 10 am till about 7 pm or 8 pm from Monday through to Saturday. Some department stores also have a late night shopping day once a week, when they open till 9 pm.

To cater to the working population, hypermarkets operate late till 9 pm or 10 pm from Monday through Saturday.

Time for Running Errands

The post office is open from 8 am to 7 pm, Monday through to Friday. On Saturday, they open for half a day till 12 noon.

Banks are usually open from 9 am to 4:30 pm, Monday through to Friday. They remain closed on Saturday.

The stock exchange (Bourse) trades from 11:30 am to 2:30 pm, Monday through Friday.

In the event of an emergency, after-hours services include:

- **Post Office**
  Open 24 hours at 52, rue du Louvre, *1er*; Tel. 42.33.71.60. If taking the *Métro,* alight at Louvre.
- **Currency Exchange**
  Open everyday from 6:30 am to 11 pm, at Gare de Lyon.

Sunday is Family Day

Sundays are a holiday for nearly everyone in France, except for the food sellers who operate on Sunday morning. This is the big market day, as Sunday midday is still the most popular time to organize a big family meal. (Often, in lieu of church.) Consequently, there will be no one about in the town or in the parks on a Sunday until about 2 pm when lunch is over. Before that, everyone is busy buying food for the meal, preparing the meal or getting dressed and driving to Granny's house to eat the meal.

The Monday Holiday

Shops that stay open on Saturday or Sunday usually close Mondays. Don't panic, at least one *boulanger* or *pâtissier* in each neighborhood will open both Sunday and Monday so the French and other croissant and *baguette* addicts can have their fresh "hit" for the day. Just don't be surprised to find many places closed on Monday.

The Year's Holidays and Seasons

Like most Europeans, the French write their dates numerically, starting with the day, then the month, then the year.

The official summer holiday in France starts on Bastille Day, 14 July, and goes through the end of August. Parisians leave town for the whole of August. Paris is very quite that month, except for the tourists.

Some people prefer this calmer version of the city. There won't be opera and other major cultural events, though the Mayor of Paris puts on special events during the summer, to compensate, but there won't be any traffic jams, either. Conversely, expect the seaside resorts and country camp-grounds to be packed to the gills.

In early September, schools begin and everyone returns to the routine. In October, usually the best month for good weather, Paris is jammed with all sorts of special events and conferences. Hotels will be booked up and restaurants will require reservations.

On the major holidays, the banks and post office will close and the long weekend will lure many families out on the highway. Fatalities rise so sharply during these periods, the government has tried to spread out the school holidays more evenly, scheduling six weeks of school followed by two weeks' holiday.

Turn to the Calendar of Festivals and Holidays for a complete listing of the festivals and holidays observed in France.

TRAFFIC AND TRANSPORTATION

French traffic is the first thing most people experience in France. It is exhilarating – or terrifying – depending on your attachment to this existence and your understanding of French rules.

The French appear to have little concern for life or property once behind the wheel of an automobile and it is a tribute to their highly developed driving skills (of which they are most proud) that more tourists and locals are not killed each year.

Not that you should relax. The French kill twice as many of each other per-driver as the British, Americans and Japanese. Though such butchery is more common on the major *autoroutes*, do be careful crossing the street, even inside the pedestrian (zebra) markers with the light in your favor.

Taxis

Your first traffic experience will probably be a ride in a Paris taxi… that should be sufficient lesson. Like other French drivers, these men and women, strapped into their beautiful new Mercedes and Peugeots, can stop on a dime, roar to 100 km/h in seconds, and judge the perimeter of their vehicle to less than a centimeter.

They use all of these techniques to maneuver through the Paris traffic. Consider yourself on a carnival ride and be grateful it's that other poor soul out there, not you, trying to cross the street. You'll be among the masses soon enough.

Taxis are expensive in Paris. There are extra charges for time and mileage, which are indicated on the meter, then a surcharge for bags put in the boot or trunk, for waiting and for evening services. Charges go up to the maximum just as the *Métro* stops. The tip expected is usually 5–7% of the fare.

But you have at the wheel a raconteur, as well as a driver, and don't be afraid to engage in serious political discussion as the fellow negotiates seemingly impossible feats of traffic ballet.

Driving

When you begin walking around Paris (the very best way to enjoy it), keep those first performances in mind. If you really insist on driving, you will need an international driver's license, plus your own country's driver's license, and you must be 18 or older. Carry insurance for your car, or pay for it when you rent one. Those centimeters can get very thin.

Top speed, officially, in Paris is 50 km/h, 120 km/h on the *autoroutes*. At intersections of equally important streets, not otherwise marked, the vehicle on the right ALWAYS has the right of way, except in a circle like the Arc de Triomphe, where the vehicles already circling take priority over those coming in. Red traffic lights get ignored regularly. When there is a green light in your favor, look before you charge out there.

Fay Sharman says the French treat their cars the way they treat women. Though I am grateful that hasn't been my experience, I must admit I actually enjoy French traffic. From the relative safety of a Paris sidewalk cafe, one can watch the confrontations, contortions and brilliant near misses with endless amusement.

185

It is something like a dance. The first rule is: the rules were made to be broken. This is particularly so with parking. There aren't enough places to park in Paris, even though most cars are quite small and there are many underground parking lots now. To compensate this squeeze, people improvise. (Remember System D? This is another example.)

The second rule of the game is: the more clever the breach of the parking law, the better the status points for the driver.

One summer evening, I dined outside at a narrow, five-street intersection in an old and congested part of Paris. Two of the five streets came together at a sharp angle, forming a triangle of extra pavement before the streets actually merged. Several small cars were wedged illegally into that space, parked, as it were, against the point of a triangle of cheese.

A tow truck was loading up and carting off the one furthest out, struggling with the limitations of the spaces involved, as we sat down to eat. (A Paris tow truck is a remarkable machine with straps that can be placed around the chassis of a car that allow it to pluck a vehicle from the most inaccessible spaces.)

As soon as the truck disappeared up the street, another car came along, parked in that spot, and the driver got out and walked away, quite pleased with his ingenuity.

A few minutes later, back came the tow truck and proceeded to load up this latest parking violator. We in the restaurant sat captivated for hours as the tow trucks and vehicles played out their ballet. The number of parked vehicles never diminished, as the "space" always filled again. Nobody ever offered to tell the vehicles' owners.

The driver would strut away with a grin of accomplishment on his face, and we would smile slyly and wait for the truck to return. It was very good drama, a modern Myth of Sisyphus, performed through the night and into eternity, no doubt by a faithful army of civil servants in Paris. It certainly inspired me to stick to my preferred mode of private transportation in Paris, the bicycle.

Cycling

From the pedestrian's perspective, the cyclist is a lunatic. But when you are on the bicycle, you only see the beautiful city in front of you, never the mad traffic jostling for position behind you. They always make room for you!

You can slip between lanes of clogged traffic and even use the bus lanes, which are limited to buses and taxis. Nobody minds. Everybody is nice to a cyclist in France, even the fast-dancing drivers of Paris.

I used to credit this to their passionate love of the sport of bicycle racing. But now I've learned there is actually a law giving two-wheeled vehicles favor over four-wheeled vehicles in a court of law. So, if an automobile hits a bicycle in France, he is apt to have to pay the damages.

You aren't supposed to hit anything or anybody in French traffic. That is really awful and causes all kinds of nuisances for everybody, but you want to be the guy with the superior position, if possible. This can involve you in things like horn-blowing contests and shouting and fist-waving with other drivers and even pedestrians.

But in all my years on a bicycle, no one has ever blown their horn, waved their fist or shouted at me. The French love their *petite reine* as they call the bicycle and they give way to her on every occasion.

As a result, Paris traffic is manageable on a bicycle, at least to an alert and seasoned urban cyclist. I recommend it, though I wear a helmet now (quite unusual in Paris) and I watch out for those most dangerous of drivers, the tourists.

The countryside of France is nothing short of magnificent on a bicycle (that is another book.) The S.N.C.F. allows you to bring your bicycle on most suburban trains and to check it into baggage when you are traveling longer distances. They also rent bicycles at most of the major train stations.

Public Transportation

The French philosophy of *égalité* really shines when it comes to moving people around on public transportation. You can go everywhere in the country by some public conveyance. In Paris, everyone of every class uses the *métro* and the buses. For that reason Paris addresses often note the nearest *métro* station with an "M:" and the name.

People are generally polite in public transport. They will hold the door for the person behind them. They will let people exit a train or bus before getting on. They will relinquish a seat to the elderly or the handicapped. Both the bus and *métro* systems are relatively easy to use, given the detailed nature of their services. The little green tickets you buy in the *métro* station (cheaper by the ten-pack or *carnet*) also serve on the buses, though a long bus ride may cost you more than one ticket whereas one ticket takes you anywhere in the *métro* system.

Some buses offer an outdoor back deck, perfect for sight-seeing and picture-taking, or just enjoying the sunshine.

Children under ten ride at half price. A first class car in the middle of some trains is reserved for first-class ticket buyers from 9 am to 5 pm but open to everyone the rest of the time. Since "no smoking" was instituted in the subways, they are cleaner and more pleasant.

Look at the maps available at bus stops and in the *métro* to figure out your route. Don't be embarrassed. Everybody does it!

On the buses you must *composter* your ticket by pushing it into a red slot that loudly punches it as "used". Buses are boarded at the front and exited in the middle. Many bus services stop at 8 pm and all buses and *métro* services stop by 1 in the morning and don't start again until 5:30. Taxis accommodate by raising their prices to maximum during these hours.

Trains in France are generally clean, fast and inexpensive. The TGV (*Trains à Grande Vitesse*) reach a maximum speed of 300 km/h and zip from Paris to Marseilles in four hours and the Eurostar goes from Paris to London in three, under the English channel. You need reservations for these trains, however, and as different ones start from different stations in Paris, be sure you get to the right station. (Remember the star pattern!)

The biggest nuisance in public transport in France is the *grève* or strike. They are usually announced in advance and the lines affected are indicated. But they can sure clog the works.

PICKPOCKETS AND THE LOST & FOUND

Pickpockets are particularly active in crowded places. Keep your valuables well buried in your clothes and watch for purposefully distracting activities such as dropping change or asking for the time which would allow a second person to rummage in your bags.

There is a central "Lost & Found" in Paris at Metro Convention, but you have to be able to prove what you lost is yours and pay a few francs, based on the value of what you lost.

Better to carry the minimum and keep it guarded. Carry some form of identification, for example, your passport, at all times. And keep copies of your birth certificate and first passport pages elsewhere among your things, just in case you lose yours. The passport is the premier thing you need for any kind of travel, anywhere. Although in France it is not actually a legal form of identification, it is generally accepted as such.

PUBLIC COMMUNICATION SERVICES
"It's the little things in life that drive you crazy."
—American poet Charles Bukowski

The Post Office – La Poste (PTT)
Nothing frustrates internationals as consistently as the French postal system, partly because we are all used to the way our home postal services work and the French system is quite unique. Suddenly a little detail of life like a stamp takes on enormous proportions and that sunny yellow sign over the post office entrance, those yellow postal boxes and yellow postal trucks, become symbols of torture.

The French postal system actually works remarkably well, considering the circular way in which everything seems to be organized. Most remarkable are the hours: open from 8 am to 7 pm Monday through Friday and 8 am to 12 noon on Saturday.

And recently they have improved their organization, though you still have to pick a window, usually, and hope that the one you picked gets you to the front of the line fastest.

These days most windows offer *tous services* or all services. But there are always a few at which some unique service is available. If you want real stamps (*timbres de collection*) for example, usually only one window has them. The rest just print out a tape and slap it onto your letter or postcard, obliterating part of your message or part of the picture on the other side if you didn't leave adequate space for it.

If you do line up at the wrong *guichet*, you will be told (usually with little sympathy) that you must go to the back of the line at another one (usually indicated by number) where the services you want are provided. Remember the star pattern? Essentially, you started down the wrong street.

If you need more than one kind of service at *La Poste*, you may need to wait in more than one line. However, these different windows will become more familiar to you in time and eventually a trip to the post office will only take 15 or 20 minutes, instead of a long, frustrating morning.

But start out feeling you have ALL the time in the world and don't get impatient!

Here are the usual choices and services:

- *Poste Aérienne*. Now there are two categories for overseas mail, *Prioritaire* and *Economique* but both go by air. You can ask for a *carte des tarifs* which gives all the charges. At many post offices there is a scale outside the service windows, so you can weigh your own letters and figure out the cost.
- Letters within Europe and the UK go at the same fees as within France first-class. All letters can be registered (*recommandé*), insured (*valeurs declarées*) or sent COD (*objets contre remboursement*). You just need to get the right forms. Letters within Paris are usually delivered by the next day and no more than a day later within France.
- *Timbres de Collection*. This is the window for buying regular stick-on stamps as well as the pretty, commemorative stamps that the PTT is continually producing. Ask for *beaux timbres* and give the franc denominations you need. They also have aerogrammes, overseas folding letters with postage printed on them, and pre-stamped domestic postcards (*cartes postales pré-affranchies*) at this window, usually on display. You will have to buy other letter-writing supplies at a stationery store. (You can also buy regular stamps at any bar, press center or *brasserie* where you see the sign *Tabac*.)
- *Paquets*. For mailing small parcels, magazines (*journaux*), books and brochures (*livres*) or other printed matter (*imprimés*), you need

to go to this window. The PTT also sells very substantial yellow packing boxes in various sizes. They are usually on display, with prices attached and you can buy them from any window. You'll need to pack it and seal it, then have it weighed at the *Paquets* window with the little green international contents sticker for customs (*la déclaration de douane*) filled out. Ask for those when you buy the boxes and be sure to describe the contents, as prices vary based on what is inside. Books and magazines, for example, get a cheaper rate. You can also insure the contents (*assuré*) at this window. Keep your packages light, less than two kilos for small packages, no more than five kilos for books and printed matter.

- *Postexpress* and *Chronopost* are the French superfast delivery services, competing with the likes of DHL and UPS, both domestically and internationally. You can send up to 25 kilos with a COD value up to 750 euros and *Chronopost* gets packages to New York the next day, after noon. *Postexpress* gets packages up to five kilos anywhere in France in 24 hours and they will pick up from your home or office (*Allo Postexpress*). Get details at the appropriate windows.

- *Postéclair* – This is the new fax transmission service offered by the PTT. Unfortunately, the person you send to cannot reply back to you by the same way.

- *Poste Restante* is the general delivery service, for people without home addresses or in need of postal boxes. This is also the "will call" window, known as *Retrait des lettres et paquets*. If you get a notice in your mail that a package is waiting for you at this post office, bring your notice, your ID and wait at this window.

- *Caisse d'Epargne. La Poste* in France functions as a bank, too. You can open an account, get a *Carte Bleue* credit card and withdraw money via the cash card machines outside many of the post offices. Inside, you can get money orders (*mandat international*) in various currencies, wire money and some post offices will even change money. You can also pay your telephone and EDF bills here. (See "Money and Banking" section.)

THE FRENCH TELEPHONE

Twenty years ago, the French had one of the worst phone systems in the world, but as often happens in France, a group of French bureaucrats applied themselves to the problem and the French phone service leapt ahead of everyone, surprising even the French. Now the phones in France work well, they are reasonably priced, and the supplemental services have greatly expanded.

It is easy to use the public phone system in France which would be excellent except for the high level of vandalism of the handsome glass boxes all over the country. Most now require the use of a card, either a debit or a credit card. The debit phonecard, the "Telecarte", is available from France Telecom, or street kiosks, metro stations, tobacco shops and post offices in a variety of values. Insert the card and the phone will automatically keep track of the value as you make your call. The speed at which the value is spent depends on the cost of the call you are making. Should the value run out, you can even insert another card, if you have it handy, without losing the connection.

To subscribe to a telephone service, be it for a landline or a cell phone, just drop into your neighborhood France Telecom office. Landlines come with a free messaging service, useful to have when you are out. You can also subscribe to a variety of independent cell phone services.

If you aren't staying long in France, you can buy or bring your own GSM (European standard) cell phone. Then buy and slip in a chip from any one of several French suppliers including Orange and SFR. You will then have your new phone number. "Time" debit cards for the phone can be purchased as you need them. Each chip supplier has his own debit card system and phone shops offer a wide range of telephone and Internet services.

Early in the 1980s, France Telecom jumped ahead the Internet Revolution with their *Minitel* monitor plus keyboard hardware. This little electronic gem was offered free, or at minimal charge, to conventional telephone subscribers. It changed the way the French communicated with each other and the world, long before anyone had heard of something called the Internet. Everyone was linking up using the *Minitel*, including embarrassingly (for France Telecom) lucrative sites that brought men and women together for specific leisure time activities.

The *Minitel* still works well though it is overshadowed by personal computers and the World Wide Web. The *Minitel* links directly to a central server by dialing into a four-digit number and connecting. The central server offers a wide variety of public and private information and services, many of them for only the cost of the phone call. (Phone calls, even local ones, have never been free in France, though some incoming cell phones services offer free incoming calls now.)

The *Minitel* is great for making train reservations. You simply dial "3615" then punch in "SNCF" on the *Minitel*. There is also a free access number to search all the phone numbers and addresses in France. This *annuaire* (directory) is reached by dialing "3611" on the *Minitel*. You can find a newer version of the *Minitel* at most Post Offices offering *annuaire* services, so you can look up contact information if you don't have a *Minitel* at home.

The latest dialing system in France is also pretty handy. Every number in France and its DOM (overseas departments such as Guadeloupe) is now a 10-digit number. Each number starts with a "0", followed by one or several numbers that indicate the geographic location and then the local number. Thus you have to dial the full 10-digit number, whether you are calling from down the street or across the country or over from the Caribbean. (You pay for the call at different rates, depending on the distance and time of day.)

If you want to make calls outside of France or to the French TOM (overseas territories such as New Caledonia), you dial two zeros, then the country code and the rest of the number. If you call into France, however, you dial the country code for France, which is 33, then drop the first "0" and dial the rest of the 10-digit number.

Installing Telephone Service

Although the PTT is also the telephone company, you don't go to the post office to order a telephone. You go to your neighborhood *Services Commerciaux des Télécommunications*. These are listed in the yellow pages telephone directory at the post office and they are usually very nice offices, again organized on a star pattern, but in this case, you start at an information (*Accueil*) desk, explaining what you need and giving your name. Then you sit down in a nice plush chair there and wait to be called. (Take a book or newspaper.)

You must show formal identification plus proof of residence, either an EDF bill in your name, or letters written to you at that address, or your rental agreement.

You then have to know: (1) what kind of plugs are installed already in your apartment, (2) how many telephones you want, and what style, whether you want to be listed in the *annuaire* (which gets you on the *Minitel* automatically), (3) whether you want a *Minitel*, (4) where you want your bill sent and (5) how you want to pay. If you pay by automatic deduction from your bank account (*prélèvement*) you need to bring proof of your bank account (*relevé d'identité bancaire*) which is usually a slip included with your checkbook. Installation usually takes just a few days.

NECESSITIES OF CLEANING UP
Toilets: The Public Ones

This subject deserves a whole chapter. Until the last decade, French public toilets were notoriously smelly old tin fence structures, where men (and men, only) could take one step off the sidewalk, pee behind this barricade, and continue walking down the street, often zipping up as they went along.

These *urinoirs* or *vespasiennes* were basically a hope into the underground sewer system, with a bit of water dribbing along with the urine. You could smell them a block away and they were entirely for the benefit of men.

No longer! The French jumped from the 19th century to the 21st with their sparkling new *Toilettes*. You'll see them everywhere in France, now, and elsewhere in the world they are cropping up. A modern plastic tubular structure, these facilities are a tribute to French ingenuity: they are spotlessly clean, nearly vandal-proof and offer complete service for men and women, including toilet paper and piped-in music.

Insert fifty (euro) cents in the slot and the handless door slides open, receding into the curve of the structure. Step inside the seamless, all white, brightly-lit cavity and the door automatically closes. Music begins. The toilet-like seat is used in the normal manner but there is no flushing to do and no apparent plumbing. Push the button to open the door when you finish and once you've stepped out, the door will close again and the entire room will be flushed and cleaned chemically, ready for the next user.

The French have gone from the ridiculous to the sublime, as far as public toilets go. These new *Toilettes* have got to be the cleanest public facilities on the planet. As with the TGV trains, they even beat Japan.

Other Toilets

Not all the toilet facilities in France match this remarkable standard of the public ones. There are plenty of smelly old W.C.'s around. For some reason, the French adopted the English term "Water Closet" or W.C., pronounced "dooble-veh-ceh" in French.

Some facilities are just that: a closet with a hole in the middle of the floor and two foot pedestals on either side. These "squat" or Turkish toilets take a bit of getting used to and years of use have seeped them deep in the predictable odors. Just hold your nose and remember that the deep squat position is anatomically correct for the

The new vandal-proof public Toilettes *offer clean and convenient facilities. The door opens when fifty (euro) cents are put in the slot. Step in, the door closes, lights and music come on. Push the button inside for the door to open again.*

activities involved.

More and more "western" toilets are in use in France, but flushing arrangements will again challenge your ingenuity. A pull chain from a reservoir over your head, a push button on the reservoir behind the bowl, a pull lever on compressed water tanks, a button to step on in the floor ... all these variations exist in France.

A further difficulty in toilets is the lighting system. Because electricity used to be very expensive in France, many energy-saving techniques were developed. One common one is in lighting the usually windowless W.C.

Sometimes the light comes on automatically when the door is closed and locked and goes off when the door is unlocked. You must risk locking yourself into a pitch dark room, of course, but if you haven't found a light switch, shutting the door and throwing the lock will probably do it.

In fancier places, or places where there is a good deal of public traffic, an attendant may be positioned at the entrance to the toilets and demand a franc for their use. In such cases, you can demand toilet paper be provided.

Privacy

Partly because of the years with the old *pissoirs*, French men are rather casual about such activities. They will often stand by a wall on the street, especially at night. It's not so bad. Since people are accustomed to cleaning up the dog leavings, this leaves just one more doggy trail in the morning.

In many restaurants and cafés, men and women share a common wash basin that is positioned between their respective toilets. A urinal may sometimes be next to the handwashing bowl, convenient for the men, but a bit awkward for the women.

In most cases, now, there will be a door marked for *Dames* or *Femmes* and one for *Messieurs* or *Hommes*. Sometimes the *hommes* forget to close the door.

Many café and restaurant patrons frown on your using their facilities, however humble they may be, unless you are a paying customer. At least buy a coffee for the privilege. Or try the public toilets.

The Private Bathrooms

Private toilets also come in various shapes and sizes, often in a room separate from the bath and wash basin. Be sure to ask for the *toilette*, not the *salle de bain*. Your hotel room will cost more if both private bath and toilet are included.

In some hotels and private homes, you will find another curious fixture, a French invention known as the *bidet*. (Pron: bee DHAY). This looks a bit like a toilet and, like a toilet, is designed to be sat upon, but is for cleaning oneself, nothing else.

A spray of warm water (you must adjust the temperature, so sit facing the faucets) shoots up from the middle of it, and in the days when weekly or monthly bathing was the norm, the *bidet* must have been the ultimate in personal hygiene.

Now that so many of us take daily showers, the *bidet* is a bit redundant, but people who like them swear by them. In old hotels in France, you will get a sink and a *bidet* in your room, but neither a toilet nor a bath. You'll have to find those somewhere down the hall.

It is very bad form to use the bidet for anything other than cleaning oneself or one's clothes. You can fill it up like a laundry sink. In fact, even doing laundry by hand is often discouraged in some hotels. Laundry dripping on the floor might leak through to the room below.

Laundry Services

Laundry service in hotels is expensive in France, as it is everywhere. The days of washing-up ladies are over. You will probably need to learn about French self-service laundries. These are efficient and inexpensive and often combined with self-service dry-cleaning.

In the old ones, you buy *jetons* to operate the machines, one *jeton*

for each machine. They can usually cope with about seven kilos of laundry. Laundry soap is also available at most self-service places, but you might want to bring bleach and softeners. Bring lots of change as usually no change is given.

In the newer places, all services are paid for from a single source. You fill your machine, deposit the money indicated and push the button with the number of your machine on it. Sometimes you must then push a button to start the machine, especially if it is the dryer.

To minimize drying time, some of these self-service places feature a *super-essorage* centrifuge machine that gives a minute's hard spin to the clothes. This machine must be used with caution, balancing the load carefully to get a good spin.

Dryers in France are very hot, so watch woolens, nylons, nylon zippers and Velcro. But they do not offer long cycles. Heavy things like jeans will take two or three cycles without the *super-essorage*.

Plan about an hour and a half, minimum, for a trip to the laundry. It's a drag. Nobody likes it.

HEALTH CARE AND SOCIAL SERVICES

There are three main branches of government services, as they relate to you and your family: health care, retirement and unemployment pensions and family allowances. Employers, employees and the state all contribute to pay for these services and even if you are not a French citizen, you have rights to any of them, for whose services you and you employer are paying.

There are both public and private health care services available. You pay directly for treatment and medicines, then you are reimbursed by the government, if you are eligible. If you are not, you should not come to live in France without some kind of health insurance, preferably one that includes repatriation coverage for returning you to your home country for extended care. You won't get a visa to live in France without your own health insurance.

The American Hospital in Paris is an English-speaking hospital in Neuilly. It is much more expensive than French hospitals, but is acceptable to most American medical insurance policies. The Hertford British Hospital in Levallois-Perret specializes in maternity cases and its staff are bilingual in English and French.

The Women's Institute for Continuing Education has a very complete book *Health Care Resources in Paris*, which is worth buying if you are going to be in France for any length of time. Copies are available at WICE.

French hospitals have a fairly relaxed pace. Doctors give patients ample stays and patients are expected to supply their own pajamas, robes, towels and toiletries ... even for their babies being born! Medicine is freely administered and the price of both medical supplies and services are government controlled.

Medicines are sold through the *Pharmacies* displaying the green cross. The people working in these shops have sufficient medical training to advise you on common medical problems. They can even provide you with prescribed medicines, based on your complaints. But if they think you should see a doctor, they can also recommend appropriate specialists in the neighborhood, both private and public. They also are responsible for explaining how to use your doctor's prescriptions, and can even advise you on whether or not the mushrooms you just found in the woods are edible!

Emergency medical care is *Service d'Aide Médicale d'Urgence* (SAMU) and the Paris number is 15. There is also a number for English-speakers operated by *S.O.S. Médecins* at 01.47.23.80.80. If your case is not life-threatening, but you are too sick to go to a doctor, there are on-call physicians who will come to your home 24 hours a day, 365 days a year, for a reasonable price, through *S.O.S. Médecins*. But look upon the local pharmacist as your first line of defense.

RENTING AN APARTMENT: WHAT TO CONSIDER

Your first job here may well be finding a place to live. Outside of Paris, this is not so difficult, but pressure for apartments in the City of Light is intense. Rents are high and spaces are small. A standard *deux-pièces* is normal for a couple ... that's two rooms, not two bedrooms plus living room and dining room. Kitchens and bathrooms do not count as rooms, for good reason; they are usually very small. Modern conveniences such as washing machines, dishwashers and microwaves may well be considered extras.

You can hunt with the rest of the Paris population to find a nice place, but you would be better off connecting with the foreign community, the American or English churches, for example. There are billboards at these organizations offering sublets and second-hand furniture by other internationals leaving town. Also check the English language publications and ask the staff at these organizations. Contact the addresses at the back of this book.

Whatever way you begin your search, here are some things to consider:

1. Neighborhood. The range of characteristics is wide in Paris, including some pretty dangerous spots up in the north of the city (the 18th and 19th *arrondissements*) where drugs are a problem. But even in these sections there are very nice areas. Rather than hunt all over town, stick with a couple of neighborhoods you like, walk through them to spot *A louer* signs in windows or look for the street names in advertisements in weekly advertising sheets like *Particulier à Particulier*.

2. *Quel étage*? The higher up the apartment, the more light and air you will have. If there is an elevator in the building, the flats high up will be expensive. If not, they will get cheaper as you go up. In older buildings, the most elegant apartments are on the lower floors. They will have high ceilings, long windows and interior details. Don't be put off by something on the 5th floor without an elevator, however, unless you have serious physical disabilities. You really do get used to climbing stairs and that extra bit of exercise will help your body compensate for the rich French meals you enjoy.

3. Noise. Paris streets are noisy. And the main roads through tiny little villages have trucks (lorries) thundering through all night. Consider your tolerance. Most French apartments have window shutters that close out noise, but they also close out light and air. Apartments opening onto courtyards, away from the street, are usually more expensive because they are more quiet, but they may be noisy if there are many apartments facing the courtyard and lots of people using the courtyard as an access. Noise ricochets up those high stone walls.

4. Mail services and *concierges*. If possible, get into a building with the old-style French *concierge* (who will probably be Portuguese,

but that doesn't matter). These women guard against nuisances like overflowing garbage, mail delivery and special notices, servicemen arriving, and they will even hold an extra set of keys to your place, in case you lose yours. They are a marvelous breed, keeping you up with gossip, with politics, and with protocol, really invaluable to the newcomer.

If your building hasn't got a *concierge*, your mailbox will be lined up inside the doorway. Make sure yours is locked. Often they are not big enough for magazines and your subscriptions will be left in a common trough. Mail tampering is a problem in Paris, so arrange for a locking mailbox big enough for all your mail.

5. Charges. You will have to pay two months' rent in advance, usually, as well as a fee to the agent. Make sure you get all the papers stating what you've paid and what you are due back at the end. See the section on "French Law in Your Life" for your legal rights as a tenant in France.

6. Red tape. France is built on a mountain of bureaucracy. It works, and some of it actually is very sensible. But speed is not the primary consideration. As with everything in France, be patient. Finding an apartment and renting it takes time.

MANAGING YOUR HOME IN FRANCE

Partners and children of people coming to France to live and do business have a peculiar set of problems which are different from the person in the family whose job brings him or her here. Having a specific assignment in one's own field of endeavor gives a person a connection to the new culture that often bridges the deepest troughs of cultural distance. Unemployed spouses and children, who must go about all of their normal activities in totally new ways often have many more culture adjustments to make.

The rule of thumb in multinational companies is that one out of three employees sent abroad come home early from the assignment.

Robert Kohls says that studies show four out of five early returns from work abroad are because the spouse, not the employee, couldn't adjust. One woman in Paris for six months explained some of her problems thus:

"My husband's company said we could bring whatever we wanted with us, so I brought everything, right down to soap and toilet paper. Although he said it was silly, that such things would be available here in France, I knew it might be difficult to find the things I wanted. For example, I forgot shampoo and spent two hours and $20 finding what I hope is equivalent to what we use at home. My husband was furious.

"As a wife here, the very things which I did at home with expertise are suddenly a whole new ball game. I have to reinvent the wheel. None of my expertise in shopping and keeping house in America applies here."

"Why didn't anyone tell us it was going to be so hard?" complains another spouse. "I came to Paris expecting a wonderful, romantic experience, and I feel lost and alone. It's much harder to find work, to find apartments, than I expected. My husband has no sympathy with my problems. I feel like an innocent victim, and it makes me angry."

Indeed, women have a special legal status here in France. Gabrielle Varro is an international living in Paris for 25 years and author of a book about international women married to French men. *The Transplanted Woman* examines a number of the problems of intercultural marriages and multicultural children. She says that knowledge of the Napoleonic Code is essential for understanding the status of men and women in France. Although new laws regarding marriage and the rights of women came into effect in the 1970s, cultures change at a slower pace. Women can expect to be treated differently in France, both legally and culturally.

Children, too, experience difficulties adjusting to a new culture. They can feel equally isolated. They have left their friends behind and must start in a new school and a new language. Usually, though, children find it much easier than adults. They imitate the new culture more readily, as they are still in the complex process of learning to imitate their own.

So expect many challenges in your new home and try to enjoy the differences as part of your expanded cultural awareness.

A Few Logistics of Home Appliances

In spite of a large number of nuclear power stations, French electricity is still relatively expensive and by tradition is considered something akin to liquid gold among the value-conscious French. Be sure to turn off lights and even unplug fixtures in hotels, as a guest in private homes, and even when at home yourself. You will pick up the habit easily as there are reminders everywhere.

In most hallways in private buildings, lights will be on timers activated by small buttons on the wall marked *Lumière*. You push the button, the lights come on. After a couple of minutes, they cut themselves off.

If you haven't reached your destination, you'll be left in the dark. At that point, you just have to find the nearest button to push (newer ones glow). If you are going upstairs, don't panic. There is usually a *Lumière* button on every level.

France is unusual in Europe, in that they still have both 110 and 220–250 voltage systems. The standard now is 220v, but in some older buildings you can find 110v. The plugs look the same, so ask before you plug in anything. A 220v appliance won't be hurt by a 110v socket, but it won't work. But a 110v appliance will be fried by a 220v socket.

If you are coming from the USA where 110v is the norm, then each of your appliances will need a step-down transformer between it and the French 220–250v wall socket.

When buying *transformateurs*, ask the man at the hardware store (*Quincaillerie*) rather than a hotel clerk or a *concierge* who may not understand multivoltage aspects of electricity. The higher wattage the transformer you buy, the more appliances you can run off of it. Just add up the wattages of the things you are plugging in and don't exceed the limit.

The standard French electrical plug is a round two-prong device, similar to the old German one but longer and thinner. Converting from two-prong flat American plugs will be easy, but bring two-prong converters for your three-prong plugs.

The wiring code is brown for live (or hot) and blue for neutral, should you need to get that far into things. Remember 220v can kill more easily than 110v.

Light bulbs (*ampoules électriques*) are either screw-in or bayonet, which take a quarter turn to release. The French use both and they are not interchangeable.

Television reception in France is the SECAM system, so your television set will probably be useless. French broadcast television quality is one of the best in the world, however. Much better than the American system, but not quite as good as Japan's, so you will enjoy having a French TV. Video players must be those that can adapt from your PAL or NTSC system to SECAM, if you want to play your video library in France.

The French use AM, FM and LW radio frequencies, but English language radio programs are available in France only on the long wave frequency (LW). You might want to leave your radio behind and buy one when you get here if yours does not include the long wave option.

Computers, on both the IBM and Macintosh standards, are readily available in France, though expensive. Bring yours with you, paying careful attention to the voltage considerations above.

The telephone system works exactly like phones everywhere except for a variation in the plug into the wall. You will find adapters for your international standard plugs readily available in large hardware stores such as BHV (pronounced Bey Hash Vey). In fact, you will find just about everything you need for around the home at BHV, a haven for do-it-yourselfers living in France.

CHILDREN AND THEIR EDUCATION

Children are naturally more culturally adaptable than adults, but when you first put them into a strange, new setting, they are going to look to you as model for their adjustment attitudes. A positive approach to your new life in France, taking it all as a new family adventure, will greatly help your children adjust.

Clinical psychologist Paul Marcille, who works with family adjustment problems in Paris, says that children will mirror their parents' attitude. Pushing kids out to adapt to their new surrounds on their own won't work. You have to start by doing it together.

Also, Marcille says, children's needs will vary depending on their developmental stage in life. A very young child will be more concerned about losing his favorite TV programs, than his friends in daycare. An adolescent, who is normally trying to establish his independence from parents and family, will miss his peer group and will probably need your support more than he is able to admit. Your sensitivity can affect your child's adjustment skills now and later on in life. Children rarely have negative reactions to a new environment unless their parents teach it to them by their own example. It has also been proven that children who learn multicultural skills early in life have a distinct advantage as adults in international settings.

Recognize the potential problems early, and seek professional help if you don't feel you can handle them. For helpful sources, please refer to the contacts and bibliography listed at the back of this book.

Education in France

As a resident paying French taxes, you can take advantage of the French educational system. If you have very young children, you are in luck! The French government offers *école maternelle* for children from the age of two until five, when they enter kindergarten for a year, then the first grade. Although these schools stop for lunch and close on Wednesdays, there are *cantines* and *garderies* to fill in the gaps for working mothers.

Don't worry about the language differences with your very young. Children below the age of nine pick up new languages as easily as their first one. Most international families who come to France quickly bow to their children's superior ability to communicate in French, even if the whole family started at the same skills level.

Once a child reaches the age of nine, however, he starts to learn languages more slowly. If you have such school-age children who do not have French language skills when they come, you might consider an English-speaking school for the first year, moving on to a bilingual school after that.

There are a number of French bilingual schools (called *bilingues*) which you might well consider as an alternative to expensive, private English-language education in France. These *bilingues* get high ratings among international students I've talked to. One bright young international I know contrasts the pretense of friendship she has found at her English-language school with the more honest, but cooler reception from classmates at the *bilingue* school. Isolating English speakers from the French community gives many children a false sense of superiority.

If your children are younger than nine or have strong French skills already and if you plan to stay in France until their education is complete, you should certainly consider a regular French school.

The Association of American Wives of Europeans has published an excellent *Guide to Education*, discussing in detail the whole subject of bilingual and monolingual education in France. It is available from the American Church in Paris or AAWE (see sources in the appendices).

In their booklet, they ask several important question you should consider when choosing a bilingual school:

• What subjects are taught in English?
• Are English classes separated by ability or just age?
• What are the students' record for further education?
• What percentage of students are multicultural?

Chapter Ten

CULTURE SHOCK IN FRANCE

WHAT IS CULTURE?

> "*La culture, c'est l'environnement tangible et intangible édifié par l'homme.*" (Culture is that tangible and intangible environment man creates.)

> —H. Triandis

Coping with someone else's culture is stressful. Yet cultural adaptation is the sometimes-painful requirement of a successful multicultural life. You cannot make the adjustments painless, but you can reduce the number of painful experiences you must endure, learn from them and enjoy the process of better understanding another culture and yourself.

For the tourist, this means a more valuable vacation. But for the professional and for the international company that has sent him abroad, the cultural adjustments we discuss in this book can mean the difference between professional success and failure.

Assigning home office personnel abroad is an expensive and complex proposition. Franck Gauthey et. al. say that when such assignees return early, unable to adapt to their new environment, they cost their company between $25,000 and $125,000 in wasted capital, not to mention the hard feelings left with clients they were unable to deal with successfully. Multinational companies need leaders who are internationally adept.

Although a little book such as this cannot describe or solve all the problems of cultural transition, we can help you anticipate them and explain some of the reasons behind the cultural differences. Since the first edition of this book was published in 1990, interest in the subject of French cultural understanding has increased enormously.

It must be the Chunnel. A half dozen new books have been written on the subject of French culture alone. We include many of them in the Bibliography and refer to some of them in other parts of this book.

In explaining some of the reasons why the French behave as they do, we hope we reduce the "strangeness" of their behavior, lessen the shock and accelerate your transition into French life, deepening your appreciation of the wonderful people of France.

People vary enormously in their ability to adapt to new environments. Your success will depend in part on your previously successful experiences outside of your own culture and in your innate tolerance for ambiguity. We guarantee it will not be painless, no matter who you are. Yet sometimes the people who find adjusting the most difficult actually do a better job of it! They suffer more, perhaps, so they search more earnestly for solutions to the problems.

In learning to cope with another culture, you will quickly recognize how deeply you are colored by your own cultural training. It is a humbling discovery to realize that much of the way we behave is actually cultural habit, not something innately individual.

What makes one way of doing things "correct" and another "incorrect" usually depends on cultural learning. It is hard for the person inside his own culture to recognize it, much less to explain it to anyone else. But once he leaves his own culture, that "correctness" starts to dissolve and he is left in a very ambiguous world.

This same someone who prides himself on his "individuality" must now come to terms with the horror that his own "unique personality" and "world-view values" include quite biased cultural baggage he will have to discard if he is going to fit into the culture now surrounding him. Whether it is enjoying food, dressing, expressing pleasure or evaluating priorities, each of us has learned to act in ways that conform to our own culture. When we move into another culture, suddenly we have to renegotiate some very basic things, things we have taken for granted since childhood.

The basis of all cultural adaptation is getting rid of one's own cultural preconceptions. Table manners, for example. The tools we use, how we use them, what we do with our arms, elbows, hands and mouths, all come as second-nature at home. So it is a shock to suddenly enter another culture where the habits are different. Many habits must now stop and new ways observed and copied, just to assume the basic requirement of "good table manners".

Ironically, cultures that appear to be just a little bit different from our own sometimes take more effort to adjust to. They take closer observation and an equally strong suspension of one's own cultural values as do very different cultures.

You might not notice, for example, that the French eat salad with their fork in their left hand, but pasta with their fork in their right hand. Your French colleagues will take offense if you do it another way at a business lunch with important clients. Likewise, the high volume of your voice in a small crowded restaurant would be a painful and awkward experience for your French colleagues in Paris, though nobody would even notice your boisterousness in New York.

Fortunately, we don't lose our ability to reconform as we get older. In fact, studies are now showing that the Golden Years often require the greatest adaptability of all. We are quite literally never to old to learn.

Adapting to a new culture is much like learning a new language. It takes daily practice and continuous intellectual effort. You have to be observant and imaginative, but patient and thick-skinned. You cannot take anything personally. Always think like a duck. Let each seemingly negative response roll right off your back. Imagining that you are being personally victimized is death to cultural understanding.

By responding positively to the challenge of cultural adaptation, by observing carefully your new surroundings, and accepting the job of learning a new way of doing just about everything, your life will be enormously enriched, both inside and outside of France.

Life is a series of re-adjustments. Living outside your own culture expands your perspectives on the world. By trying to get comfortable in other cultures, trying to learn other ways of doing everything, you learn much more about "yourself". That is what makes an international experience so valuable.

Cultural adaptation is a challenge. If you don't rise to the challenge, you miss the rewards of it. Like physical fitness, being culturally adaptable takes a kind of exercise and results in a state of fitness. The more you practice, the better you get at it. The more you understand and "fit" into another culture, the broader your world becomes.

What is Culture Shock?

Culture shock is only one part of cultural transition. Culture shock was described by P. Bock in 1970 as "primarily an emotional reaction that follows from not being able to understand, control and predict another's behavior."

213

Dr. Kalervo Oberg, an anthropologist who defined the term "culture shock" in 1960, says culture shock is brought on by "the anxiety that results from losing familiar signs and symbols of social intercourse."

Considered among the founding fathers in the field of cross-cultural communication, Oberg defined several aspects of culture shock for the United States Agency for International Development. To briefly summarize Oberg's findings, there are at least six aspects of culture shock:

1. Strain due to the effort required to make necessary psychological adaptations.
2. A sense of loss and feelings of deprivation in regard to friends, status, profession and possessions.
3. Being rejected by and/or rejecting members of the new culture.
4. Confusion in role, role expectation, values, feelings and self-identity.
5. Surprise, anxiety and even disgust and indignation after becoming aware of cultural differences.
6. Feelings of impotence due to not being able to cope with the new environment.

The Stages of Culture Shock

The pseudo-medical model of cross-cultural stress was developed first by Oberg and others and still is used today. Oberg's model is combined with the U-curve approach, developed about the same time, and described in detail in the book by Adrian Furnham and Stephen Bochner, *Culture Shock: Psychological reactions to unfamiliar environments*.

In the curve, the visitor starts with elation about the new culture, drops down into a trough of depression and confusion, then comes back up with a sense of satisfaction and optimism. This curve can happen many times, in varying intensity and over a varying period of time, but the cycle itself is now considered a normal reaction, though both mental and physical illness may be apparent. Using this model, we create a typical six-month cycle of attitudinal, emotional and physical responses you may have to France, or any other country which you visit for an extended period of time.

Pre-Departure

"I'm so excited! Paris, here I come."

Activities	Planning, packing, processing, partying and parting.
Attitudes	Anticipation of new and interesting things. Lessening interest in current responsibilities.
Emotions	Enthusiasm and excitement, mixed with concern for leaving friends, relatives and a familiar environment. Children are particularly apprehensive and uncomfortable.
Physical response	Adults and children running on nervous energy. Difficulty sleeping.

The First Month

"Isn't it wonderful? Even more beautiful than the pictures."

Activities	Welcoming and introductions. New foods, sights, sounds and people. Start learning the language, realizing it's necessary.
Attitudes	Curiosity about the culture and the various opportunities. Downplaying the negative comments of other expatriates, the inability of waiters to understand you.
Emotions	Euphoria. You are really in France and it is really so beautiful.
Physical response	Some problems with all the food and wine, the condition known as *crise de foie*, a kind of hangover effect from too much rich butter,

215

cream and fat in the diet. Some difficulty sleeping in a new place, with new night noises.

The Second Month

"This post office eats my letters."

Activities	Moving into a permanent residence. Full job responsibilities and settling into a routine.
Attitudes	The charm of the tiny apartment and the exquisite menus of local restaurants start to look different. Growing awareness of what is not available, or what is ridiculously expensive. Impatience with "rude" waiters and "indifferent" shopkeepers.
Emotions	Nervous, uncertain about how to function. Some withdrawal from the French, and seeking the familiar in friends and food.
Physical responses	Colds and the flu (especially in winter). Gaining weight.

The Third Month

"I like France but I don't like the French."

Activities	Language skills hit a plateau and seem to stop improving. People still don't understand you and work keeps you too busy to study, anyway. Work performance declines.
Attitudes	Discouraged, irritable, hypercritical. Negative cultural value judgements predominate. Conversations turn into long strings of complaints, stereotypical truisms seem confirmed.
Emotions	Depressed, discouraged and suspicious of strangers. Very lonely. Culture shock in extreme.
Physical response	Extreme fatigue, often illness.

The Fourth and Fifth Month

"You know, this is actually a very efficient way of doing it!"

Activities	Small victories in work and language study. Ways of getting things done are sorted out. Moments of competency bring hope. (If this does not begin to happen during this time, the visitor will usually give up.)
Attitudes	Constructive and positive in outlook and potential. Accommodation to the French ways of doing things begins.
Emotions	Renewed interest in France and the French.
Physical response	Health restored.

The Sixth Month:

"Your first visit? Well, don't miss ..."

Activities	Routine established and visits now planned into other parts of the country with visiting friends. Local friendships established.
Attitudes	Maintain basic constructive attitude despite good days and bad days. Plateau reached.
Emotions	The ups and downs of life now accepted as normal, and a growing interest in helping others and reaching out to those who are struggling.
Physical response	Normal.

Many aspects of individual personality and experience profoundly affect this basic formula. Your "cycle" may be quite different, but few people will be able to learn much about their new culture without experiencing troughs of negative feelings and discouragement. Cultural stress can have profound negative effects on people, but it need not be treated as a disease.

S. Bochner has developed a culture-learning model to deal with culture shock that looks for solutions by learning cultural characteristics that apply. Appropriate cultural skills are survival skills, in a way. Without them the international attracts attention to himself as an outsider. Proper awareness, preparation and attitude can help the international accumulate these skills.

HOW TO DEVELOP CULTURAL AWARENESS

Furnham and Bochner describe several training techniques for developing social skills, and thus minimizing culture shock:

1. Information-giving. This book is all about that and many more sources follow in the Bibliography.

2. Cultural Sensitization. Real adaptation comes from observation, but there are ways you can fine-tune your observational skills. The first step is recognizing that invisible difference between you and another person: cultural perspective. The Bloom Program, a course offered each October by the Women of the American Church in Paris, integrates cultural sensitization with basics on dealing with Paris. Details are available from the American Church and WICE.

3. Understanding the reasons behind actions or attributes of another culture. One of my chief inspirations in researching this book the first time was a book by French anthropologist Raymonde Carroll called, in English, *Cultural Misunderstanding*. Her wisdom is scattered throughout this book and helped me enormously in understanding why the French do what they do, something they themselves often cannot describe. While few of us can aspire to be the talented social scientist Dr. Carroll is, I'd like to quote her five steps for developing cultural understanding:

   a) Clear the deck. Avoid all attempts at discovering the deep-seated reasons for the cultural specificity of such-and-such a group. Although psychology, geography, history, religion and economics may be part of what people "really are", these do not deal with the culture. Just seek to understand the culture, the system of communication.

    b) Be on the lookout. Listen to your own discourse, making judgements about people. "The French are ..." No. "I find the French to be like this or that ..." Yes. What is true is: another culture does not have the same characteristics as yours. Try to avoid judging these differences as good or bad.

    c) Recognize a "cultural test" which is a sense of strangeness and unpleasantness, opacity in a certain situation. And remember the situation in as much detail as possible, before judgement has given it a broad stroke. Listen and watch with complete attention.

    d) Then analyze the experience to find an interpretation that can be verified elsewhere in the culture.

    e) Finally see, from this analysis, how other aspects of the culture might apply.

4. Learning informally from "old-hands" on site is another suggestion of Furnham and Bochner. It's informal and some information from old hands is better than others, but it always helps to discuss your observations with others familiar with your problems.

5. Formal Social Skills Training aimed at cross-cultural competence. This you will find in the next section on training in cultural awareness.

Is It Really Possible to Be Multicultural?

Yes! More and more work is being done in the field of multicultural life. Marriages, children, work and retirement are increasingly multicultural. There is a common comparison between learning a culture and learning a language, with as many stages of "fluency" along the way. Multicultural expertise takes practice, but people can speak and act in more ways than one. They eventually do it subconsciously.

My favorite example of this was a large group of Chinese whom I observed queued up properly with me at Heathrow Airport for one of the first nonstop flights to Hong Kong. I was impressed by their

"Britishness" and made a mental note to myself as we boarded the plane in a very orderly way. But when we landed at Hong Kong's Kai Tak Airport the wheels had hardly touched the tarmac before this same group were up and grabbing their luggage from the overhead bins, headed for the exit. While the cabin attendants managed to get them seated safely again for the taxi into the terminal, you can bet I was knocked aside when that door finally did open. Hey, welcome to Hong Kong!

The biggest pitfall to multicultural understanding is assuming that cultural differences don't matter. The mediums of TV and cinema can change dress codes and language in an instant, but real cultural values change remarkably slowly. Businesses gearing up for the European Union are far more aware of this now than when they started.

An international in Paris

The ability to fly about the planet quickly and cheaply does not diminish the cultural differences into which we debark. It is much easier to get there, but it still takes time and effort to become culturally functional and years to feel truly "at home". But a multicultural life is possible. We are all cultural chameleons, eager to "fit in" wherever we are.

When I finish this book, I leave my *pied-à-terre* in France for a weekend with my mother in the home of my childhood on the East Coast of America. Then I fly to my own home in San Francisco. From there I continue on to Japan where I have a magazine story assignment. In Tokyo, I stay with my Japanese "family", who have hosted me dozens of times in the past. Finally, just two weeks after leaving Paris, I land in Hong Kong, where I will spend the summer writing about Asia from a small island "home" I return to each year.

In each stop I will be dealing with different friends, different cultures and different jobs. In each I must be able to function and communicate, both professionally and socially. I must rely on previously learned skills, because the flight schedule allows me no time to learn new ways. With my subconscious of appropriate cultural habits and the generous support system of friends and acquaintances I have established previously in each of these places, I will feel "at home" in each of these places.

Don't be surprised to see me among those Hong Kong returnees pushing my way off the plane next time, either!

Cultural adaptation is something like riding a bicycle: once you learn cultural techniques, they start to become subconscious, second nature. To the extent that I can function well as an international, I am multicultural. I am not multilingual, except at the most primitive levels, but I am at a comfortable level of multicultural skills. This allows me to make short visits with ease, and longer visits give me the chance to learn more.

Unlike riding a bicycle, there's always plenty of room for improving and refining intercultural skills! The general rule is: the more closely you observe and study another culture, the more you will learn.

Professional Help in Cultural Transitions

In addition to the many aspects of cultural differences and cultural awareness considered in this book, there are formal psychological and linguistic approaches now being developed to these "invisible realities". Both before your departure and after you arrive in France, you will find experts in the multi-disciplined field of cultural transition which may be of great help.

L. Robert Kohls identifies four formal approaches to cross-cultural preparedness: (1) education, which provides broad content knowledge of the subject country; (2) training, which focuses on performing specific skills or meeting specific objectives effectively; (3) orientation, which prepares a person to understand and function in another culture; and (4) briefing, which provides a broad overview of a culture.

Aspects of numbers (1),(3) and (4) are included elsewhere in this book and refer you to a number of resources, all included in the Bibliography. Many people are practising and developing number (2), cross-cultural training. Two good sources of both people and literature in this field are:

Society For International Educational Training and Research (SIETAR)
733 15th St. NW, Suite 900
Washington DC 20005 USA
Tel: 202-296-4710

They have a scholarly journal, a newsletter and networking services to other members and organizations, as well as a book catalog available on request. Also,

BCIV Institute of American University
3301 New Mexico Ave NW
Washington DC 20016 USA

The field of cultural awareness has blossomed in the last decade. Just be sure you get specifics on France!

Choosing an Intercultural Trainer

We can only scratch the surface of the problem of cultural adaptation in France with this book. If you are planning to do business in France or coming to live in France for any reason, it would be well worth your while to get some intercultural training.

Kohls, again, offers some basic guidelines for choosing an international trainer who, he says, should have all the following qualifications:

1. Personal knowledge of France and at least two years of living experience there.
2. A positive attitude towards France and French people.
3. The experience of having lived through culture shock, somewhere.
4. A fundamental knowledge of the basic values of your home culture.
5. Experience with stand-up training and experiential learning techniques.
6. Interest in both content and process training.
7. An image that is acceptable to the people being trained.

Turn to the Resource Guide for a wide range of resources on culture and language.

GOING HOME … CAN YOU GO HOME AGAIN?

"What in the world is the matter with you? You've always loved my charcoaled hamburgers."

Experienced cross-culturalists will tell you that the hardest part of the international experience is usually the return home. Though you never can totally integrate into another culture and though you may not have enjoyed the effort of trying, you will almost certainly find reintegrating into your first culture a difficult transition.

It is clear that we adapt to other cultures in both conscious and subconscious ways. Re-adapting to our former cultural "norms" takes a surprising amount of conscious effort. The changes we have made to adjust to something different are not really reversible. Even if you conscientiously resist another culture, you pick up new habits in spite of yourself. We human beings can't help being conformists, and in the case of France, the temptation to conform to French ways is overwhelmingly positive.

Going home is another complex cultural transition, a new relationship to an old cultural setting. Expect this part of your international experience to take from six months to a year. I have met many people doing business internationally who find going home the most difficult transition of all. They call it a kind of reverse homesickness. The cultural shock, the pain, is related to the unconsciousness of cultural response. Suddenly, what you do naturally doesn't work. There is an invisible brick in your path.

The closer the culture is to your own, the more likely you are to be caught unawares. France, for another Westerner, ought to be an easy adjustment but it isn't. Going home ought to be easiest of all. Surprise! It is the hardest. When you examine them, the problems of going home are obvious. You are out of touch with local news and gossip. Yet it isn't so interesting now, in your new context. Your old friends, however, cannot imagine or recognize the changes you have made. They are expecting the old you, with the old values and habits of home. They will be quickly bored by tales of your life abroad, even though they will express interest at first. Their lives revolve around a different center and that is the center they expect to share with you.

Your descriptions of life in France will soon be judged as "bragging". Don't compare the French cuisine you've come to love to the barbecue your friends have prepared for your return, even if favorably. You have seen enough of your friends' vacation photos and home movies to know how well yours will go over with them. Likewise, any complaints you have about how difficult things were abroad will be taken very lightly.

"You were lonely in Paris? Are you kidding?"

"What do you mean the Paris office is very formal? They seem quite relaxed when they visit us."

You have changed, sometimes in ways you didn't even know. This will intimidate everyone, even you. Just be prepared for it and give yourself and your friends the patience and understanding you have learned to use abroad with strangers. You have another cultural adjustment to make, and it takes patience and conscious effort.

Back at the Home Office

Your company will be one in a thousand if it expresses any interest in the "expertise" you've gained in working at the French branch. They figure the French locals are the experts. You were just a go-between. You're back; the job's done. The next person assigned to Paris will go through all the painful learning experiences you did. And those bridges you painstakingly built between yourself and the Paris staff will be meaningless to your boss who has never needed them.

This opacity towards international business relations is changing. Companies are starting to develop sensitivities to the invisible aspects of international relations. They are beginning to recognize that language is not enough, that the synergy of business relations requires deep intercultural understanding. Increasingly, internationals, like yourself, will be called to make the different applications of company policy work. The heterogeneous aspect of international life is a source of richness, if used properly, as Franck Gauthey et. al. have said.

The expanded view of the world that the international brings to the office also makes certain local aspects of the job less satisfying. But such expansion is essential in international living and international relations, both in business and in politics. You are just the messenger, but expect to take a bit of heat for it, and don't despair, your message is important.

CULTURAL QUIZ

Situation 1

An evening at a good French restaurant is planned with friends who are visiting Paris for the first time. You've made reservations and arrive a bit late to find the *maître d'* cool and the waiters unfriendly. Your guests complain that French people are rude. Do you:

A. Agree with your friends and concede that this is just another example, making a good evening in spite of it by laughing with your friends at the supercilious attitude of the staff?

B. Ignore your friends' comment and apologise for being late and strive all evening to make up for it to the restaurant staff?

C. Interpret the attitude at the restaurant as normal and brush off your friends' comments?

D. Strive to explain to your friends about the Paris waiter's rudeness game and show him how to play it, in return?

E. Attempt through your serious interest in the wine and cuisine to win over the waiters and prove your friends wrong?

Comments

This situation comes up so many times in Paris, it should be in every guidebook. French waiters are professionals; they take their work seriously and with pride. By recognizing them as professionals, you can avoid the emotional reaction of feeling rejected by their coolness, and teach your compatriots to take the French attitude towards food. So, option E is the most productive, though you can still enjoy your evening with your friends by ignoring the situation, which makes you appear rude, in turn, to the restaurant staff and reconfirms their view that foreigners don't appreciate French cuisine or behave properly in public and should be enjoyed as sport and pleasure.

Situation 2

You've just moved into your apartment and you need to order telephone service/plumbing repairs/electrical service. Do you ...

A. Call the company and try to make arrangements over the telephone?

B. Visit your nearest Telecom office, plumber or EDF shop and ask them for the service you need, in person?

C. Contact the *gardienne* or *concierge* in your building and ask them to handle the job for you, expecting to pay a handsome tip.

D. Ask your secretary at work to handle these details.

227

Comments

In France, people tend to do their own chores, and there is little crossover between personal and private life. Your secretary will not expect to have such private matters in her hands. Although the *gardienne* in your building could help you with some details of private life, you will find things happen most expediently when you go, in person, to the office or service company you require. It is usually more difficult to get anything like services, train reservations and specific information accomplished over the telephone. Projects such as the telephone service installation will take some time, standing in lines, filling out forms and showing identification. Take along all your documents and have all your questions ready in advance. Remember, only your specific questions will be answered and few helpful suggestions will be volunteered. Treat the person helping you as you would treat a stranger giving requested assistance. Expect less than enthusiastic response to your dilemma. Take some reading material, to occupy your time while waiting. Be patient.

Situation 3

You have just arrived at the company offices where you will be working in Paris. You have already met most of your fellow workers on previous visits. Now you are coming in as a "local" staff member, yourself. A group at the office is going to lunch and invite you to join them, but once at the restaurant the conversation turns to politics, and a roaring argument develops, in French. Your reaction is:

A. To sit in shock, unable to eat, fearing physical violence will erupt at any moment.

B. Realize that your new French friends have turned their back on you, speaking quickly in French to one another without regard for your limited language skills. Assume you are an outsider and expected to sit quietly by while they discuss the details of their own political situation.

C. Vow to improve your language skills so that you can participate, and follow the conversation closely.
D. Make your comments, if you understand the gist of the conversation, even if you can only express yourself in English, when there is a lull in the conversation and you see a chance to jump in without interrupting.
E. Scold the group for being far too heated on the subject of politics and try to turn the conversation back to English and to matters of business that are on your mind.

Comments

Many French people love to discuss and debate, especially on the subject of politics. Debate, itself, is an art form, in France, and their

English skills may not be sufficient for such parrying. So resign yourself to French, during the lunch hour, often to heated debates, especially on the subject of politics. Your growing skills in the language, and growing knowledge of French politics will make these experiences more interesting. They are a vital part of living in France.

Situation 4

You are invited to dinner with French acquaintances. It is for 8 pm and you arrive early to an elegant apartment, with a bottle of white wine which needs chilling. You offer to put the bottle in the refrigerator and ask where the kitchen is. Your hostess takes the wine, leads you to the living room, instead and keeps you there until dinner is served in the dining room. After the meal, you depart the same way you came in, feeling you've been treated too much as a stranger and not enough as a friend. You wanted to see the whole apartment! Do you:

A. Assume that you have been given the "cold shoulder" and refuse their next invitation as insincere?

B. Confront your acquaintances and ask them what you did "wrong", but find they don't seem to understand your question?

C. Feel distanced from these people but reciprocate your hosts' efforts, nonetheless, with a dinner at your favorite restaurant. In that environment, they appear to be more open and friendly.

D. Return to your hosts' home and expect, this time, to be entertained only in the living room and dining room, recognizing that your presence in the house is already a display of intimacy, even if the rest of the house is off limits.

E. Confront your hosts in the first place and ask to see the house when you first arrive.

Comments

The French do not make a habit of "showing off" their house to first-time guests. It would be considered boastful as well as too intimate.

Plus they probably haven't got the rest of the house looking as perfect as the part they intend for you to enjoy.

So if you really want to see the house, ask in advance of your arrival, to give them time to prepare it for you properly. Otherwise, if you are not invited to take a look around it, don't ask yourself into any room that is not shown to you (except of course the toilet, which you can ask for!). Accept this modesty and don't mistake it for haughtiness.

Situation 5

You are on the street looking for a certain gourmet food shop you thought was on that block but isn't. Your time is short and you've left the address at home. You ask which of the following people for help:
A. A policeman ambling down the street?
B. A businessman with a briefcase briskly walking the same way?
C. An older woman in black bent over and moving slowly towards the *métro*?
D. The *métro* ticket seller?
E. A fashionable, well-dressed woman of middle age waiting for the light?

Comments

Choosing the person from whom you ask directions in France is very important, when seeking a good answer. Unless your question involves traffic law, don't seek the help of a policeman, or anyone else in uniform. They do not consider it their job to direct either locals or foreigners, and they often do not speak English, anyway. The same with the *métro* ticket seller.

Giving directions is not part of his job. A person with a brisk walk may well be in a hurry, best not to interrupt him, as a proper explanation may take time and patience he isn't currently able to give. Finally, an older woman in black is probably from the countryside and may not know the area well, plus she certainly wouldn't be frequenting gourmet food stores. It's best to choose the person most likely to frequent the shop and least preoccupied with other duties.

Situation 6

You are included in your first business meeting at work. Your boss acts as chairperson and he requests progress reports on a specific project from various members of your teams dealing with different aspects of the job. To your surprise, as each person's turn comes, he or she seems full of complaints and problems to report, often turning blame for the situation on your boss. Your turn comes. Do you:

A. Take the same pose, presenting your situation as too difficult and demanding help from your boss?
B. Pass, leaving your report unsaid?
C. Give the report you had planned to give, outlining the current situation but without any criticism or complaint?
D. Turn to other members of the group whom you feel have unfairly criticized the boss and explain your criticism?

E. Assume that your boss is just about to be fired and you'll be looking for another job tomorrow?

Comments

Meetings in France have a function similar to luncheon discussions. Members participating are expected to be critical and discriminating in their observations. Although they may appear to be putting blame on the chairman's head, such comments are more an opportunity for the speaker to exhibit his command and skill in his job.

The chairman will not take honest criticism personally, but he will listen critically, as all others in the room are expected to do. So, it will not be your job to defend your boss. He does not feel threatened. It will be your job, however, to sharpen up your report to convey your own skills at discerning both negative and positive aspects of your particular situation. A sweetened version of the facts will not impress the boss with your skills. It may be taken as a false compliment. Better to prepare a sharp, observant report in advance.

Situation 7

You have established certain shops in your neighborhood as your regular stops. One day, when you are in a hurry with a long shopping list, the lady who sells you cheeses begins a long explanation of the day's specials and then begins a story about a pickpocket who was apprehended by an angry victim on the street corner the previous day. You can see the story is going to take some time and you don't want to be held up indefinitely. Do you:

A. Interrupt the speaker, explain that you are in a hurry, and ask for your bill?
B. Let her finish her story and then express regret, followed immediately by "how much do I owe you?"
C. Console the lady about the growing violence on the streets and confirm that active victims get better results than the police force, then say you will return for your packages later?

Comments

Relationships, both in business and personal life, are critical in France and being in a hurry is hardly considered sufficient grounds for denying your acquaintances the chance to express their concerns and convey exciting neighborhood gossip. People you do business with regularly, especially those shopkeepers in your neighborhood who recognize you as a regular, will make a special effort with you, as a valued customer. Such conversation is one of the ways they establish that intimacy and give special treatment. By brushing them aside, you destroy the delicate bridge of friendship that they are building. However, we all get in a hurry at times, so by apologizing for your hurry and making a special effort with that shopkeeper the next time you are buying, you can avoid damage to the relationship.

DO'S AND DON'TS
APPENDIX

DO'S

- Do say *Bonjour, Madame* (etc.), *Merci, Madame* (etc.) and *Au revoir* to any person with whom you are making any exchange in a shop or on the street. This includes everyone from the checkout clerk at the *supermarché* to the postman.
- Do respond to the comments of the shopkeepers and expect a conversation with them, even a lengthy one.
- Do use *Madame, Monsieur* and *Mademoiselle* when saying hello and goodbye to colleagues and professional acquaintances, along with a handshake to each.
- Do respect the privacy of your neighbors.
- Do dress sharply and hold yourself as if you are proud of who and what you are.
- Do speak just loudly enough to be heard and never enough to disturb other people.
- Do hold the door open for the person behind you.
- Do try to respond to someone's request for directions, or stay with them until someone else can be stopped and asked for help.
- Do ask for information and assistance from any public person as you would ask for a favor from a stranger. Never assume it is their job!
- Do ask people for whom they voted in the election and beef up on your political understanding of France.
- Do return a compliment or positive comment with an expression of appreciation and respect for that person's judgement. "Oh, do you think so?" asked honestly, is your best response. Don't deny

a compliment, as it is given in sincerity and should not be rebuffed.

- Do watch carefully, in conversation, for signs of boredom, or the desire of your listener to speak. Be ready to change topics at any time.
- Do expect serious and heated discussions in business meetings and dinner conversations, but don't take criticism and differing opinions personally.
- Do learn as much French as possible before you arrive, and use it, even if you are not sure of your grammar and vocabulary.

DONT'S

- Don't respond to comments or solicitations from strangers, including "the look".
- Don't make eye contact with strangers on the street.
- Don't walk down the street smiling at everything. People will assume you are mentally feeble and possible dangerous.
- Don't strike up conversations with strangers of the opposite sex, unless it is to give or get directions.
- Don't use first names unless the person also knows and uses your first name and is your age or younger.
- Don't volunteer the prices of things you have bought unless you are among intimate friends.
- Don't ask what someone does for a living.
- Don't ask about a person's family or a person's age unless you are on intimate terms and they have asked you similar questions, already.
- Don't make a compliment just to be polite.
- Don't open a closed door without knocking first. But don't wait for a reply before entering. A knock means "I'm coming in", in France.
- Don't follow your host around the house. Stay out of the kitchen and don't even pour yourself a drink, unless invited to do so.

GLOSSARY

LANGUAGE

The most common stumbling block to making oneself understood in another language is pronunciation. Don't be afraid to imitate the people around you. Try to speak with the local accent, even if you feel self-conscious or foolish.

Generally, when we aren't completely confident in our speaking abilities, we tend to emphasize our own peculiar way of pronouncing words in order to maintain an element of familiarity in a situation where everything else is strange and foreign. This may make you feel more comfortable, but it won't help others understand you.

Thinking of yourself as an actor or actress playing a role is a good way to surmount these inhibitions; it also is a good way for both you and the person with whom you are speaking to have some fun!

French Basics

Hello – *Bonjour; Salut*
Do you speak English? – *Parlez-vous anglais?*
Yes – *Oui*
No – *Non*
Goodbye – *Au Revoir; Salut*
Please – *S'il vous plaît; S'il te plaît*
Excuse me – *Excusez-moi; Pardon*
Thank you – *Merci*
You're welcome – *Je vous en prie; Je t'en prie*
OK; I see – *D'accord*
I don't understand – *Je ne comprend pas*

Could you speak more slowly? – *Est-ce que vous pouvez parler plus lentement?*

I don't know – *Je ne sais pas*

How do you say this in French? – *Comment dit-on ça en français?*

What's your name? – *Comment vous appellez-vous?*

My name is… – *Je m'appelle…*

I come from… – *Je viens de(s)…*

How are you? – *Comment-allez vous? Ça va?*

Great, thanks! – *Très bien, merci!*

I'm doing OK, and you? – *Ça va, et vous?*

Oh really? – *Ah bon?*

Of course – *Bien sûr*

As you please; as you like – *Comme vous voulez; comme tu veux*

Where? – *Où?*

When? – *Quand?*

Why? – *Pourquoi?*

Who? – *Qui?*

How? – *Comment?*

How many; how much? – *Combien?*

Useful Words and Phrases

addition (f.) – the bill

apéritif (m.) – before dinner cocktail

arrondissement (m.) – district, of which there are 20 in Paris

Assemblée Nationale (f.) – the French parliament

baguette (f.) – traditional long, thin Parisian bread

bar (m.) – small café

bar à vin (m.) – wine bar

bibliothèque (f.) – library

bien élevé – well brought up

billet (m.) – ticket

boucherie (f.) – butcher shop

boulangerie (f.) – bakery

brasserie (f.) – large café serving food throughout the day
café Américain (m.) – watered down espresso
café au lait (m.) – espresso with milk
café crème (m.) – espresso with cream
café noir (express) (m.) – shot of espresso
carafe d'eau (f.) – a carafe of tap water served with meals in a restaurant
carnet (m.) – discounted book of ten métro or bus tickets
carrefour (m.) – intersection; also giant supermarket
carte bleu (CB) *(f.)* – credit/debit card
carte de résident (f.) – residence permit valid for ten years
carte de séjour (f.) – residence permit valid for one year
carte d'orange (f.) – monthly public transportation pass valid in Paris
caution (f.) – security deposit
chambre (f.) – room
charcuterie (f.) – deli; specialized deli meats such as pâté or saucisson
château (m.) – castle, mansion
chaud(e) (mf.) – hot
coiffeur (m.) – hairdresser
commissariat de police (m.) – police station
concierge (mf.) – door keeper; caretaker
cuisine (f.) – kitchen
département (m.) – county
digestif (m.) – after dinner liqueur
distributeur automatique de billets (m.) – ATM machine; see also *point d'argent*
douche (f.) – shower
eau (f.) – water
église (f.) – church
Énarque (m.) – graduate of the ENA, top political university in France
enguelade (f.) – quarrel
entrée (f.) – first course; entrance
épicerie (f.) – corner store

escalier (m.) – stairway
étage (m.) – floor, story
étranger (m.) – foreigner
femme (f.) – woman
foie gras (m.) – specially prepared goose liver
fonctionnaire (m.) – civil service employee
froid(e) (mf.) – cold
fromagerie (f.) – shop selling cheese
gardien(ne) (mf.) – door keeper; caretaker
gare (f.) – railway station
grand magasin (m.) – department store
grandes écoles (f.) – most prestigious schools in the French university system
homme (m.) – man
hôtel (m.) – aristocratic town house; hotel
hôtel de ville (m.) – city hall
jardin (m.) – garden
journal (m.) – newspaper
kiosque (m.) – news stand
librarie (m.) – bookstore
location (f.) – rental
mairie (f.) – town hall
marché (m.) – market
métro (m.) – subway
Minitel (m.) – "online" computer system available to France Telecom subscribers
musée (m.) – museum
pain (m.) – bread
pâté (m.) – pork or duck based meat spread
pâtisserie (f.) – shop selling pastries and cakes
place (f.) – square
point d'argent (m.) – ATM machine
poissonnerie (f.) – shop selling fresh seafood

pont (m.) – bridge
porte (f.) – door
salle de bain (f.) – washroom
salon de thé (m.) – teahouse; upscale version of a café
sens unique (m.) – one way street
tabac (m.) – shop selling cigarettes, phonecards, stamps, etc.
toilettes (f.) pl. – toilets
vache (f.) cow (popular animal appearing in many endearing French expressions)
vin (f.) – wine
zinc (m.) – the bar, where one stands in a café

Warnings & Signs
Attention! – Careful!
Entrée – Entrance
Sortie – Exit
Ouvert – Open
Ferme – Closed
Poussez – Push
Tirez – Pull
Issue de Secours – Emergency Exit
Entrée Interdit – Do Not Enter
HS/En Panne – Out of Order
Défense de Fumer – No Smoking
Renseignements – Information
Correspondance – Transfer (Métro)
Soldes – Sale

Acronyms
* AOC (Appelation d'Origine Contrôlée)
  Agricultural, alcoholic or dairy products which meet specific standards of production are labeled thus, indicating high quality.

- EDF (Électricité de France)
  French public electricity providers.
- GDF (Gaz de France)
  French public gas providers.
- PACS (Pacte Civil de Solidarité)
  New civil solidarity agreement allowing unmarried couples, both gay and straight, to enjoy the same privileges as married couples.
- RER (Réseau Express Régional)
  Subway passing through Pariswhich also serves the surrounding suburban communities.
- RATP (Régie Autonome des Transports Parisians)
  Paris' public transportation system.
- SAMU (Service d'Aide Médicale d'Urgence)
  Public ambulance and emergency medical services.
- SNCF (Société Nationale des Chemins de Fer Français)
  French railway system.
- TGV (Train à Grande Vitesse)
  High speed long-distance train.

CALENDAR OF FESTIVALS
AND HOLIDAYS

If a national holiday falls on a Tuesday or Thursday, many companies will *faire le pont* (make a bridge). This means they will include Monday or Friday as part of the holiday as well, thus creating a four-day weekend. Take note not to plan business meetings on these days.

Here are the official and unofficial holidays:

PUBLIC HOLIDAYS

- **January 1 – Jour de l'an** (New Year's Day). New Year's Eve is usually celebrated with friends, fireworks and parties. The Eiffel Tower and Champs Elysées are two of the more popular places to be for the big countdown.
- **March/April – Lundi de Pâques** (Easter Monday). A religious holiday. Children usually have an Easter egg hunt.
- **May 1 – Fête du Travail** (Labor Day). An international celebration of workers' rights.
- **May – Victoire 1945** (French Liberation Day). Commemorated with a veterans' parade in celebration of the end of WWII.
- **April/May – Ascension** (Ascension Thursday). A religious holiday, observed on the sixth Thursday following Easter.
- **May/June – Pentecôte** (Pentecost). A religious holiday. Second Monday following Ascension.
- **July 14 – Fête Nationale** (Bastille Day). Fireworks and parades are held in the streets on Fête Nationale, in celebration of the French Revolution. There is also *La Balle de Quatorze Juillet,* an evening dance held outdoors throughout France.
- **August 15 – Assomption** (Assumption). A religious holiday.

- **November 1 – La Toussaint** (All Saint's Day). Traditionally, people bring flowers to the graves of their ancestors.
- **November 11 – Armistice 1918** (Veteran's Day). A day held in remembrance of those who fought in WWI.
- **December 25 – Noël** (Christmas). Christmas is usually celebrated with an extended family dinner (usually starting at 10 pm) on Christmas Eve. Gifts are exchanged on Christmas Eve or Christmas Day.

CULTURAL HOLIDAYS AND FESTIVALS

- **January 6 – La Fête des Rois** (Epiphany). Epiphany was originally a religious festival celebrating the visit of the Magi to Jesus. Today, the popular custom is to hide a small figurine inside a cake (*galette des rois*). The cake is then cut into pieces and distributed among the members of the family, the person with the figurine in his piece, will be king or queen for the day. *Galettes des rois* can be found in *boulangeries* throughout the week of the festival.
- **February – Mardi Gras**. Also known as *Carnaval*, the celebrations vary depending upon which part of France you visit. In several cities, such as Dunkerque, the traditional costume parade is still held. Children often have their faces painted as part of the celebrations.
- **March – Foire du Trône**. A temporary fairground is set up in the Bois de Vincennes in Paris, with rides and activities for children.
- **End of April – La Foire Internationale de Paris**. A large week-long fair held in Porte de Versailles, with vendors selling everything from furniture to food.
- **June 21 – Fête de la Musique**. An outdoor music festival held in celebration of summer. Musicians from all over the world descend upon France to play in the streets. Make sure you bring an instrument!
- **Mid November – Beaujolais Nouveau**. This is the time when the Beaujolais nouveau is officially distributed for sale throughout France. many people go out to cafés or restaurants to celebrate and savor the much-loved French wine.

OTHER NOTABLE EVENTS

• **May – French Open Tennis Championship**. Also known as *Roland Garros,* the biggest names in professional tennis come to Paris each year to compete in this event. It's the only major tennis championship held on clay courts.

• **July – Tour de France Cycling Championship**. The famous three-week cycling race across France. For information on the current year's route, go to http://www.letour.fr

• **Mid September – Les Journées du Patrimoine**. This is observed throughout the country with historic landmarks being open to the public for free admission. This includes buildings usually closed to the public, such as *le Palais de l'Elysée* (residence of the President of France).

• **Mid October – International Contemporary Art Fair (FIAC)**. Some of the greatest contemporary art works, which are privately owned, are put on display at the FIAC. Some may be available for sale.

RESOURCE GUIDE

EMERGENCIES & HEALTH

Emergency Numbers
In an emergency contact the following numbers:
Fire: 18
Ambulance (SAMU): 15
Police: 17
SOS Medecins (in English): 01.47.23.80.80
(An organization which provides 24-hour house calls.)
Crisis Hotline (in English): 01.47.23.80.80

Hospitals
There are two hospitals catering to English speakers in Paris, both
located in the suburbs to the west:
American Hospital of Paris
63 blvd Victor-Hugo; 92200 Neuilly; Tel: 01.46.41.25.25
Will accept Medicaid and most American insurance policies. However, it is much more expensive than other local hospitals.

Hertford British Hospital
3, rue Barbès; 92300 Levallois-Perret; Tel: 01.46.39.22.22
Specializes in maternity care.

Doctors
The Australian, British, Canadian, and U.S. embassies, as well as the
American Hospital, all have listings of registered English-speaking
doctors and dentists within France.

Pharmacies

Most medicine in France requires a prescription. Several pharmacies serving English speakers can be found in Paris. As most pharmacies close at the end of the working day, it's a good idea to know the location and phone number of the nearest 24-hour pharmacy in case of an emergency.

British and American Pharmacy

1, rue Auber; 75009 Paris; Tel: 01.47.42.49.40

La Pharmacie Anglaise

62, ave des Champs Élysées; 75008 Paris; Tel: 01.43.59.22.52

Pharmacie Anglo-Américain

6, rue de Castiglione; 75001 Paris; Tel: 01.42.60.72.96

Dental Clinics

For emergency dental care contact:
American Hospital of Paris (listed above)

Hôpital Hôtel Dieu

1, place du Parvis-Notre-Dame; 75004 Paris; Tel: 01.42.34.82.34

SOS Dentaire

87, blvd du Port Royal; 75013 Paris; Tel: 01.43.37.51.00

Facilities for the Disabled

In general, France does not have a lot of resources for those who are disabled. To find out more about facilities in your area, ask for information at the local town or city hall (*la mairie*). Alternatively, there are also several organizations listed below which you can go to for information.

Comité National Français Liaison Réadaptation Handicapés
236 bis, rue Tolbiac, 75013 Paris; Tel: 01.53.80.66.66

FAVA (Franco-American Volunteer Association for the Mentally Retarded)
24, rue d'Alsace-Lorraine, 75019 Paris; Tel: 01.42.45.17.91

RATP Voyages Accompagnés
21, blvd Bourdon, 75004 Paris; Tel: 01.49.59.96.00
Free door-to-door service.

TRANSPORT & COMMUNICATIONS

Telephone Service Numbers
Telephone services: 14
French directory assistance: 12
International directory assistance: 003312 + country code
Minitel directory information: 3611
Phone problems: 1013

International Telephone Calls
International calling cards are available wherever local Telecartes are sold. They generally offer good rates for calling overseas. There are also heavily discounted calling cards available for sale in certain stores in the 13eme, 18eme and 19eme. If you already have a calling card plan via your telephone company in your home country, you can use the access numbers listed below:
AT&T: 08.00.99.00.11
Australia Optus: 08.00.99.20.61
Australia Telstra: 08.00.99.00.61
British Telecom: 08.00.99.00.44
Canada Direct: 08.00.99.00.16

MCI: 08.00.99.00.19
Sprint: 08.00.99.00.87

Accessing the Internet

Both AOL and Compuserve are international Internet Service Providers (ISPs) that have local access numbers in Paris. If you don't have an account with either of these companies, there are plenty of French *fournisseurs d'accès* (providers) to choose from. Here are several of the more widely used ones at the time of publication:

Club Internet
http://www.club-internet.com; Tel: 01.55.45.45.00

Easynet France
http://www.easynet.fr; Tel: 08.11.25.70.00

Free
http://www.free.fr
A free ISP which is quite popular.

Liberty Surf
http://www.libertysurf.com
Another popular free ISP.

Wanadoo
http://www.wanadoo.fr; Tel: 08.01.63.34.34
Wanadoo is the ISP offered through France Télécom.

Cybercafés

If you don't have access to the web, you will might want to stop in at a cybercafé occasionally. In addition to Internet access, coffee and tea, some cybercafés offer word processing, scanning and printing services.

Baguenaude Café
30, rue de la Grande-Truanderie, 1er; Tel: 01.40.26.27.74

Café Orbital
13, rue de Medicis, 6eme; Tel: 01.43.25.76.77

Clicktown
15, rue du Rome, 8eme
http://www.clicktown.com

Cyber Cube
12, rue Daval, 11eme; Tel: 01.49.29.67.67 (main branch)
http://www.cybercube.com
Has four locations in Paris.

Easyeverything
31–37, blvd de Sebastopol, 1er; Tel: 01.45.86.08.77
Has branches in over 15 cities.

Web Bar
32, rue de Picardie, 3eme; Tel: 01.42.72.66.55

Free Internet services can also be found at the Centre George Pompidou, the Vidéothèque de Paris, and on avenue de Friedland near the Charles-de-Gaulle-Étoile. Be prepared to wait in line.

LANGUAGE & CULTURE
Cultural Centers and Classes in France
No matter what your native culture, you are going to need help in France and most sources for assistance here are open to everyone who speaks English. There are hundreds of them. Below we include a list of primary resources. These will lead you to the others.

Cultural Resources in English, French and Asian Languages
Alliance Française
101 blvd Raspail, 75006 Paris (M: Raspail); Tel: 01.45.44.38.28

The American Chamber of Commerce
156 bd Haussmann Tel:01.56.43.45.67
Various services for members; also library. Open Tuesday to Thursday from 10 am to 12:30 pm for non-members and *Minitel* services available at CECOM on 3617 for the public.

The American Church in Paris
65 Quai D'Orsay, 75007 Paris (M: Invalides); Tel: 01.40.62.05.00
Many programs and publications in addition to ecumenical religious services. Publishes *The Free Voice* monthly newspaper in English for the Paris community.

The American Cathedral (Episcopal)
23 ave George V, 75008 Paris; Tel: 01.53.23.84.00

American Embassy
2 rue St. Florentin, 75001 Paris; Tel: 01.43.12.22.22;
Website: www.amb-usa.fr

American Express
11 rue Scribe, 75009 Paris (M: Opera); Tel: 01.47.14.50.00

The American Library in Paris
10, rue du Général Camou, 75007 Paris; Tel: 01.53.59.12.61
Open Tuesday–Saturday, 10am–7 pm;
Website: www.americanlibraryinparis.org

The American University of Paris
31 ave Bosquet, 75007 Paris; Tel: 01.40.62.06.00
Website: www.aup.edu

The Association of American Wives of Europeans
34 ave de New York, 75116 Paris; Tel: 01.40.70.11.80;
Website: www.aaweparis.org
Programs for women living in France plus two excellent resources,
Guide to Education and *Living in France: Job Hunting, Divorce,
Retirement, Wills & Inheritance.*

Association Culturelle Franco-Japonaise
8-12 rue Bertin Poirée, 75001 Paris; Tel: 01.44.76.06.06;
Website: perso.wanadoo.fr/asstenri

Association France-Etats-Unis
9, blvd Suchet, 75016 Paris; Tel: 01.45.27.80.86

Australian Embassy
4 rue Jean-Rey, 75015 Paris; Tel: 01.40.59.33.00;
Website: www.austgov.fr

Brentano's (English language bookstore)
37, avenue de l'Opéra, 75008 Paris (M: Opera); Tel: 01.42.61.52.50

British and Commonwealth Women's Association
8 rue de Belloy, 75116 Paris; Tel: 01.47.20.50.91

The British Council
9 rue de Constantine, 75007 Paris; Tel: 01.49.55.73.00; Fax:
01.47.05.77.02; On *Minitel* at 3615

British Embassy
35 rue du Faubourg St. Honoré, 75008 Paris; Tel: 01.44.51.31.00;
Website: www.amb-grandebretagne.fr

The British Institute in Paris
11 rue Constantine, 75007 Paris; Tel: 01.44.11.73.73;
Website: www.bip.lon.ac.uk

Canadian Embassy
35 ave Montaigne, 75008 Paris; Tel: 01.44.43.29.00;
Website: www.amb-canada.fr

CAPEC (Centre Asiatique pour la Promotion Economique et Commercial)
75 ave Marceau; Tel: 01.45.63.33.54

Centre Culturel Chinois
78 rue Dunois, 75116 Paris; Tel: 01.56.89.81.00

Centre Culturel Coréen
2 ave d'Iéna, 75016 Paris; Tel: 01.47.20.83.86

Centre Culturel Franlasie
44 rue René Boulanger, 75010 Paris; Tel: 01.42.38.37.88

Commission Franco-Américaine d'Echanges Universitaires
9 rue Chardin, 75016 Paris; Tel: 01.44.14.53.60

France USA Contacts
26 rue Bénard, 75014 Paris; Tel: 01.56.53.54.54
Monthly publication for English-speaking people in France. Available from WICE, the American Church and other outlets.

Galignani (English language bookstore)
224 rue de Rivoli, 75001 Paris; Tel: 01.42.60.76.07

Indian Embassy
15 rue Alfred-Dehodencq, 75016 Paris; Tel: 01.40.50.70.70

Indonesian Embassy
49 rue Cortambert, 75016 Paris; Tel: 01.45.03.07.60

Irish Embassy
4 rue Rude, 75116 Paris; Tel: 01.44.17.67.00

Japanese Embassy
7 ave Hoche, 75008 Paris; Tel: 01.48.88.62.00

Korean Cultural Center
2 av d'Iena, 75016 Paris; Tel: 01.47.20.83.86

L'Astrolabe (maps store)
46, rue de Provence, 75009 Paris; Tel: 01.42.85.42.95

Malaysian Embassy
32 rue Spontini, 75016 Paris; Tel: 01.45.53.11.85

New Zealand Embassy
7 ter rue L. deVinci, 75116 Paris; Tel: 01.45.01.43.43; Fax: 01.45.01.43.44

Pakistan Embassy
18 rue Lord-Byron, 75008 Paris; Tel: 01.45.62.23.32

Paris Notes, The Newsletter for People Who Love Paris
P.O. Box 15818, North Hollywood, CA 91615; Tel: 800-677-9660; Website: www.parisnotes.com

People's Republic of China Embassy
11 ave George V, 75016 Paris; Tel: 01.47.23.34.45

Philippine Embassy
4 ham Boulainvilliers, 75116 Paris; Tel: 01.44.14.57.00;
Fax: 01.46.47.56.00

St. Michael's Church (Anglican)
5 rue d'Aguesseau, 75008 Paris; Tel: 01.47.42.70.88

Shakespeare & Co. Book Store
37 rue de la Bucherie, 75005 Paris (M: St. Michel); Tel: 01.43.26.96.50

Singapore Embassy
12 ave Square Foch, 75116 Paris; Tel: 01.45.00.33.61

South Korean Embassy
125 rue de Grenelle, 75007 Paris; Tel: 01.47.53.01.01;
Fax: 01.47.53.71.49

Sri Lankan Embassy
16 rue Spontini, 75016 Paris; Tel: 01.55.73.31.31

Taiwan Embassy – ASPECT
78 rue Université, 75007 Paris; Tel: 01.44.39.88.30;
Website: www.roc-taiwan-fr.com

Thailand Embassy
8 rue Greuze, 75116 Paris; Tel: 01.47.04.32.22

Vietnam Embassy (Cultural Services)
62 rue Boileau, 75116 Paris; Tel: 01.44.14.64.00

The Village Voice Bookstore
6 rue Princesse, 75006 Paris (M: Mabillon); Tel: 01.46.33.36.47

W.H. Smith (English language bookstore)
248 rue de Rivoli, 75002 Paris; Tel: 01.44.77.88.99

Women's Institute for Continuing Education (WICE)
20 blvd Montparnasse, 75015 Paris (M: Duroc); Tel: 01.45.66.75.50;
Website: www.wice-paris.org
Part of the American University in Paris, the WICE conducts courses and programs for the English-speaking; also an excellent guide to health services in France. Open Monday–Friday from 9 am–5 pm.

French Language Schools

There are numerous language schools and organizations throughout France offering French classes for foreigners. They vary in price, class size, teaching method, and elective classes offered. It's best to choose a school after having done a bit of research, as the variations are (almost) endless. Whether you want to study gastronomy, literature, or French for the workplace, you should be able to find one that suits your needs.

Listed here are some of the more popular schools. You can look through FUSAC or other English language publications for information on other schools, language exchanges or private tutors.

Alliance Française

101, blvd Raspail (Main Branch); 75270 Paris (6eme); Tel: 01.42.84.90.00; email: info@alliancefr.org; http://www.alliancefr.org;
Alliance Française can be found in many cities throughout France. They generally have decent teachers and a fair price, although the class size (22 max.) can be intimidating for some. The resource library, language lab and cultural events are among the many perks.

Berlitz

15, rue Louis le Grand (Main Branch); 75002 Paris; Tel: 01.42.66.68.15; http://www.berlitz.com;

Berlitz has 16 schools located in France, six of which are scattered throughout Paris. They teach languages "instinctively" in small groups or individual classes. More expensive than other schools, it's good for businessmen or women who would like to learn the language quickly. They also offer translation services.

Cours de Civilization Française de la Sorbonne

47, rue des Écoles; 75005 Paris; Tel: 01.40.46.22.11
http://www.fle.fr/sorbonne/

Probably the most rigorous language classes offered in Paris. This school uses a traditional teaching method with an emphasis on written texts and history of literature, as well as regular tests on grammar and vocabulary. Class size is generally between 15 and 25.

Institut Catholique de Paris

21, rue d'Assas; 75006 Paris; Tel: 01.42.22.41.80
email: sic@icp.fr; http://www.icp.fr

The Institut Catholique receives high marks from its students. The focus is on both written and oral French, and the teachers often include interesting cultural anecdotes in the learning process.

Institut de Langue Française

3, ave Bertie Albrecht; 75008 Paris; Tel: 01.45.63.24.00
email: ILF@inst-langue-fr.com; http://www.inst-langue-fr.com

Medium size classes (max. 15) for all levels. Focusing on introducing French culture as well as language, the Institut de Langue Française has a wide range of options ranging from business French (available evenings) to French cooking.

Institut Parisien
87, blvd de Grenelle; 75015 Paris; Tel: 01.40.56.09.53
email: info@institut-   parisien.com;   http://www.institut-parisien.com
Institut Parisien offers new courses weekly for students of all levels, with a class size limited to 12. Additional classes include French cuisine, fashion, literature and civilization.

ENTERTAINMENT & LEISURE

Most cities in France offer a wide range of entertainment possibilities, from major international art and music festivals to local cultural (and culinary) celebrations. Needless to say, if you're in Paris, there will never be a shortage of things to do, whether it be the cinema, the latest exhibition at Beaubourg, the opera or rollerblading along the Seine on a Sunday afternoon. Depending on what you are in the mood for, you will be sure to find it in some form or another—as long as you know where to look!

Cultural Activities

The two Paris weeklies, *Pariscope* (http://www.pariscope.com) and *l'Officiel des Spectacles*, can be bought for a minimal price at any *kiosque* in town. Inside you'll find listings for every movie, theatre and opera performance, museum exhibition and music concert playing for the week, as well as activities for the kids. A relatively new weekly, *Zurban* (http://www.zurban.com), includes detailed reviews and articles, in addition to the information listed above. The English language publications *Time Out: Paris* (http://www.timeout.com/paris) and the *Paris Free Voice* (http://www.parisvoice.com) also list a selection of major events around town.

Outside of Paris, check the weekend sections in the local newspapers for listings of both cultural and sports events. Also, take a trip to the local *mairie* for a list of tourist attractions in the area.

Eating Out

When in France, do as the French do…and take time out to enjoy the local cuisine! *Le Guide Rouge Michelin* (*The Red Guide*; http://www.viamichelin.com) and *Gault-Millau* (French–http://www.gaultmillau.fr; English–http://www.gayot.com) are probably the two most renowned restaurant guides in France. Don't, however, be intimidated into believing that their standards are the only standards. (Your savings account will regret it!) As you've no doubt discovered by now, the French are an opinionated bunch, especially when it comes to food. Ask around, see what everybody has to say! Word of mouth and an adventurous spirit continue to be the most successful combination for finding great places to eat. If all else fails, *Time Out: Paris*'s Web site (http://www.timeout.com/paris) offers some inspiring choices as well.

Classes, Clubs & Sports

The local *la mairie* (town hall) will have information on classes, clubs, sports facilities and activities in the area in which you live. There is usually a small pamphlet, which you can pick up for free, listing this information. Note that each *arrondissement* in Paris has its own *mairie*.

To find a gym or health club, look under *Clubs de Remise en Forme* in the yellow pages (http://www.pagesjaunes.fr). An extremely popular form of exercise/transportation at the moment is rollerblading. On Sundays in Paris, the *quais* are closed to motor traffic, and the cyclists and rollerbladers take full advantage of the extra space.

If football (soccer) is your thing, you're in luck. Look in *L'Equippe*, the daily sporting news, for upcoming matches. In Paris, the home team, Paris-Saint Germain, plays at the Parc des Princes in the 16eme.

Shopping

Many designer brand names such as Chanel, Louis Vuitton, and Yves Saint Laurent were born in Paris. While you might not be making too many purchases in the *haute couture* boutiques, they do make for some great shopping excursions.

The most well-known districts for clothing are:

Place des Victoires (1er): *Haute couture* designer boutiques.

St. Germain des Prés (6eme,7eme): Classy boutiques a step down from the designer stores.

Rue de Rivoli (1er, 4eme): More classy boutiques.

Les Halles (1er): Ubiquitous but familiar chain stores such as Gap or Esprit.

For American food and groceries, try the following:

Thanksgiving Grocers (4eme): 14 rue Charles V. Tel: 01.42.77.68.29. Stocks American-style groceries.

The Real McCoy (7eme): 194 rue de Grenelle. Tel: 01.45.56.98.82. Stocks American-style groceries and cooking utensils.

There are also several department stores to be found in most major cities throughout France, including: **Galleries Lafayette**, **Le Printemps**, and **La Samaritaine**. For more detail on shopping in Paris, try http://www.paris-touristoffice.com.

Bars and Clubs

For reviews of the scintillating bars and clubs of Paris, check the monthly magazines *Nova* or *Les Inrockuptibles* (both available at kiosques), *LYLO* (available at clubs throughout the city) or *Time Out: Paris*. There are also a number of English/Irish pubs to be found around town. Look through *FUSAC* for ads or check out http://www.parispubs.com, an online guide to bars in Paris.

Gay/Lesbian

The French government is one of the most supportive of gay rights in the world. The recent passage of the *Pacte Civil de Solidarité* (commonly referred to as PACS) allowing unmarried couples—both straight and gay—to enjoy the same economic and social privileges as married couples, is among the first of its kind in the world. Paris also hosts the largest Gay Pride Parade in Europe each year.

For information on the gay community in Paris, pick up a copy of one of the following magazines: *Têtu, Lesbia,* or *Gay Pied Hobdo.* The Centre Gai et Lesbien (3, rue Keller, 11e; Tel: 01.43.57.21.47), and the Maison des Femmes (163, rue de Charenton, 12e; Tel: 01.43.43.41.13) serve as meeting places and publishers for various groups in Paris. They are both good spots to meet people and find out more about local organizations and activities.

You might also want to visit *le Marais* (3e, 4e), the largest gay neighborhood in Paris. Many bars and clubs are located in this area. For more information in English on nightlife, go to the website of *Time Out: Paris* (http://www.timeout.com/paris).

RELIGION

Religious Institutions

France is traditionally a Catholic country, although at present less than 12% of the population attends church services regularly. In most major cities, you will also be able to find Protestant, Jewish and Muslim centers of worship.

For the latest information on Christian and Jewish services in English in Paris, grab a copy of *FUSAC*. For information on Muslim services, visit the Grande Mosquée in the Latin Quarter, 2, bis place du puits de l'Ermite, 75005 Paris, or try http://www.mosquee-de-paris.com.

ENGLISH LANGUAGE PUBLICATIONS

The following publications can be picked up free of charge through-out Paris at tourist attractions, language schools and the American Church in Paris.

FUSAC (France USA Contacts) – Classified ads of all kinds, from employment to personals.

Paris Insider's Guide – Practical guide for internationals who have recently arrived in Paris.

Paris Voice – A collection of reviews of cultural activities, including books, art, music, and theatre.

Time Out: Paris – Lists major events around town. Includes helpful maps and reviews of the city by *arrondissement*.

The following newspapers and magazines can be found at most *kiosques* in major cities throughout France.

- *The Economist*
- *International Herald Tribune*
- *Time*
- *The Wall Street Journal Europe*

- *Financial Times*
- *Newsweek*
- *USA Today*

Helpful Websites

For general information online, take a look at the following websites:

Work & Business
http://www.ccip.fr
Website of the Chambre de Commerce et d'Industrie de Paris, the French chamber of commerce. Contains information on starting a business in France.

http://www.paris-anglo.com
For practical information on living and working in Paris. Also posts a message board.

http://www.euro.ecb.int
A website of the European Central Bank and the national central banks of the Euro area. Provides information and updates on the euro.

News & Information
http://www.expatica.com/france
Catered specially to the English-speaking expatriate, the site is updated with local and international daily news articles.

http://www.pagesjaunes.fr
French yellow pages, in both French and English.

Food & Leisure
http://www.fromages.com
A website dedicated to traditional French cheese. All you ever wanted to know about this gourmet item. Includes suggestions for wine/cheese combinations.

http://www.paris.org
The *Paris Pages* website has a great selection of links to the monuments and museums of Paris.

http://www.paris-touristoffice.com
The official tourist guide to Paris. Provides information on children's activities, shopping, nightlife and more.

BIBLIOGRAPHY AND FURTHER READING

"There is help for those who wish it. Those who say they don't need it may be too blind to recognize the problem. The irony is that they need the help most of all."

—Robert T. Moran

When the first edition of this book was written, there were very few other titles geared to help you deal with the complex social aspects of life among the French. Now, I am happy to say, there are many. While everything you read about France in general and about cultural transition in general will help, our bibliography and recommended reading list now includes an extensive collection of books geared specifically for your life as a foreigner in France. Many of these should not be missed, especially if you are planning a long stay.

The French Today

An American in Paris by Genet (Janet Flanner); also *Men and Monuments* originally published by *The New Yorker* magazine.

Darlinghissima: Letters to a Friend by Janet Flanner, edited by Natalia Danesi Murray (Harcourt, Brace Jovanovich, 1985).

The Europeans by Luigi Barzini (Simon & Schuster, 1983).

Europeans by Jane Kramer (Farrar, Straus & Giroux, 1988).

France Today by John Ardagh (Penguin, 1988).

The French by Theodore Zeldin (Pantheon, 1986).

The Identity of France by Fernand Braudel. Translated by Sian Reynolds (Collins, Harper & Row, 1988).

An Intimate History of Humanity by Theodore Zeldin (Harper Perennial): Zeldin, through the life stories of twenty-five French women, has written a sort of history of human emotions. A fascinating insight not only into modern French life, but humanity's collective memory as well.

A Little Tour Through France by Henry James is considered a classic now, and the French haven't changed that much, especially in the countryside.

Paris Notes: A newsletter for people who love Paris. Monthly. Manhattan Beach CA.

Paris to the Moon by Adam Gopnik (Random House): This collection of entertaining and thought-provoking essays examines the nuances of French/Anglo cultural differences, touching on everything from puppet shows to the "parallel paper universe" of French bureaucracy.

The People of Paris by Joseph Barry (Doubleday & Co., 1966).

The Rules of the Game by Nathan Leites. Translated by Derek Coltman (University of Chicago Press, 1969).

Food & Film

A Food Lover's Guide to France by Patricia Wells (Workman, 1988). Also her *Food Lover's Guide to Paris*, both of them excellent restaurant and food guides, approaching the subject of eating from any number of perspectives.

The French at Table by Rudolph Chelminski (William Morrow and Company, Inc., 1985).

French Regional Cooking by Anne Willan (Hutchinson & Co. [Publishers] Ltd., London. Marshall paperback edition. 1983).

The French Through Their Films by Robin Buss (Unger, 1988).

Paris La Nuit Sexy, 20th edition, 1989. Editions Edicart's SARL, 63 rue de la Prévoyance, 94300 Vincennes. Tel: 43.65.73.70. More than you want to know of the seamy side of French life.

How-to Help for Internationals in France

At Home in Paris, Caroline Robert, editor (Published by the Junior Service League of Paris, 1993). The most exhaustive guide to the details of living in the capital city.

Bloom Where You're Planted by the Women of the American Church in Paris. Annually produced in October, they have passed their 25th year. Excellent for people just coming to live in Paris.

Buying a Home in France by Vivienne Menkes-Ivry (Simon & Schuster, 1993).

Coping with France by Fay Sharman (Basil Blackwell Inc., 1987)

Cultural Misunderstandings: The French-American Experience by Raymonde Carroll. Translated by Carol Volk (The University of Chicago Press, 1988). (Original title: *Evidences Invisbles*, Editions du Seuil, 1987.)

European Customs & Manners by Nancy L. Braganti and Elizabeth Devine (Meadowbrook, Inc., 1984).

France-USA Contacts, a monthly available from the American Church in Paris.

France: What to Know & Expect by Betty Springer (Peanut Butter, 1988).

French or Foe? by Polly Platt (Culture Crossings, 1994). A very personal and enthusiastic tour of the French cultural personality by a well-connected American who has lived in Paris for decades and specializes in cross-cultural consulting for businesses.

The French Way by Ross Steele (Passport Books, 1995). Organized alphabetically by subject from accents to xenophobia, the book offers 85 explanations in about as many pages.

Guide to Education, compiled and edited by Anita Tassel and Carolyn White-Lesieur. Published by the Association of American Wives of Europeans (AAWE), Paris. 1987.

Health Care Resources in Paris, published by the Community Health Care Committee of the Women's Institute for Continuing

Education at the American College in Paris. 1989. Revised regularly.

How to Europe by John Bermont (Murphy & Broad, 1986).

Living in France, director of publication Carolyn White-Lesieur. Published by AAWE. 1993. Includes *Job-Hunting in France* by Pamela Perraud; *Divorce in France* by Carla Potok; *Retirement in France* by Michaux, Gillet & Besson; and *Wills and Inheritance* by Persis Gouirand.

Living, Studying, and Working in France by Saskia Reilly and Lorin David Kalisky (Owl Books): A practical guide to getting situated (taxes, work permits, networking) in France.

Paris Inside-Out by David Applefield and his team at Paris-Anglophone. 1995. Also a website at **www.paris-anglo.com**

The Transplanted Woman by Gabrielle Varro. A Study of French-American Marriages in France (Praeger, Westport CT, 1988).

When in France by C. Sinclair-Stevenson (Touchstone Books, 1989).

Working in France by Carol Pineau & Maureen Kelly (Frank Books, 1991).

A Year in Provence and *Toujours Provence* by Peter Mayle. Mayle is unique. He teaches you to love the French and laugh while you learn.

French History & Literature

Antigone, Becket, The Rehearsal or any of the other plays of Jean Anouilh, the world's most performed playwright today.

Candide by Voltaire (François Marie Arouet). 1759. A philosophical novel examining life's difficulties and evils at the time of the Enlightenment in France. The time we give to something makes it important, Voltaire said, so it is wise to judge carefully how we use our time.

Diderot: The Virtue of a Philosopher by Carol Blum (The Viking Press, 1974).

The Ethics of Ambiguity by Simone deBeauvoir, lifelong companion of Jean Paul Sartre, the great 20th century existentialist. The two of them believed that man's life is totally his own responsibility, though he tries to absolve that by creating other forces and causes, such as religion.

Les Grands Auteurs Français du Programme by André Lagarde and Laurent Michard, (Les Editions Bordas). A summary series of French literature, by century, in French.

The Little Prince by Antoine de Saint-Exupéry, also written in the 1930s, found popularity all over the world. Espouses the French concept of the nobility of man which began with Voltaire.

The Marquis de Sade by Geofrey Gorer (Liveright Publishing Corp., 1934).

Les Misérables by Victor Hugo. 1862. A social novel conveying simple, humanistic ideals.

Napoleon III and the Rebuilding of Paris by David H. Pinkney (Princeton University Press, 1958).

Richelieu and the French Monarchy by C.V. Wedgewood (Collier Books, 1962).

The French Language

Thousands of books exist to teach you the language. Among them, you might take a look at the less orthodox ones.

Merde! and *Merde Encore!* by Genevieve, Angus & Robertson (UK).
Street French by David Burke (John Wiley & Sons).

Culture Shock in General

It is comforting to see that culture shock has become a serious field of study in international business, as well as sociology.

Acts of Identity by R. le Page and A. Tabouret-Keller (Cambridge University Press, 1985).

Cultures in Contact: Studies in Cross-cultural interaction, edited by Stephen Bochner (Pergamon Press Ltd., 1982).

Culture Shock: Psychological Reactions to Unfamiliar Environments by Adrian Furnham and Stephen Bochner (Methuen & Co. Ltd, 1986). Good bibliography on the subject.

The Hidden Dimension, The Silent Language and *Beyond Culture*, all by Edward T. Hall (Anchor Press, Doubleday, 1977).

Intercultural Training: Don't Leave Home Without It by Robert Kohls (SIETAR International, 1984).

International Management, a monthly magazine published by McGraw-Hill House, Maidenhead, SL6 2QL Berkshire, England. Tel: (0628) 23431.

Language Contact and Bilingualism by Rene Appel & Pieter Muysken (Edward Arnold, 1987).

Leaders Sans Frontiers by Franck Gauthey et. al. (McGraw-Hill, 1988).

Managing Cultural Differences by Philip R. Harris and Robert T. Moran. (Gulf Publishing Co., Revised 1987).

Training for the Multicultural Manager and *Training for the Cross-Cultural Mind* by Pierre Casse (SIETAR, 1984).

Venturing Abroad: Europe by Robert T. Moran (International Management/McGraw-Hill, 1989).

General Guides

MAPS are what is needed most in France. There are several excellent series produced by the National Geographic of France, the Institute Géographique National or IGN. Their maps are available all across the country and they have a major retail outlet just off the Champs Elysée in Paris. I find these more "readable" than the more famous Michelin guides, but *chacun à son goût* (each to his taste).

If you are driving in Paris you will need a map showing the one-way (*sens unique*) streets. The Relais et Châteaux folks also produce good maps.

AUTHOR

 Sally Adamson Taylor is the product of two distinct American cultures. Her father was from New York and her mother from Richmond, Virginia. Though the war between the states ended before her grandparents were born, she knew that struggle well, from both sides.

She grew up in Baltimore, Maryland, bounced between the North and the South, and learned early that at least part of any "reality" is a question of cultural perspectives. Thus she took readily to journalism and served as Managing Editor of the *Boston University News* in the late 1960s. After a year vagabonding through Europe and North Africa, she was hooked on the international life. She settled for a while in California, working her way "up" from reporter to editor to publisher, then decided that the first job suited her best.

Her home base is still a Victorian cottage in San Francisco though she has spent the last two decades living and working as a foreign correspondent with perches in Paris and in Hong Kong. She has written for a wide range of publications, including *The Asian Wall Street Journal* and *The International Herald Tribune.* She is currently Far Eastern Correspondent for *Publishers Weekly.*

CONTRIBUTOR

Christopher Pitts played a major role in sourcing for information during the updating and revision of this book. During the five years between his first and second trip to France, he was either living in China, or studying Chinese. Nevertheless, he was never able to completely shake the mysterious feeling that France might be his true home. Acting on a hunch, he finally packed up his calligraphy brushes, moved to Paris, and began his first serious study of the seemingly incomprehensible Gallic world. Following several years working in the US, Chris has returned to France, where he lives today.

INDEX